THE JOY OF

Pasta

JOE FAMULARO & LOUISE IMPERIALE

BARRON'S

Woodbury, New York · London · Toronto · Sydney

Credits

Photography:

  The color photographs are by Matthew Klein
  Food stylist, Andrea Swenson
  Prop stylist, Linda Cheverton

  Silver by Buccellati, Inc., 46 East 57th Street, New York, N.Y.
  China and crystal from Ginori, Inc., 711 Fifth Avenue, New York, N.Y.
  Linens from Pratesi, Inc., 829 Madison Avenue, New York, N.Y.
  Flowers by How, 171 West 23rd Street, New York, N.Y.

Jacket and cover design: Milton Glaser, Inc.

Book design: Milton Glaser, Inc.

All inquiries should be addressed to:
Barron's Educational Series, Inc.
113 Crossways Park Drive
Woodbury, New York 11797

Library of Congress Catalog No. 83-10025

International Standard Book No. 0-8120-5510-1

Library of Congress Cataloging in Publication Data

Famularo, Joseph J.
      The joy of pasta.
      Includes index.
      1. Cookery (Macaroni) I. Imperiale, Louise. II. Title.
TX809.M17F35 1983   641.8'22   83-10025
ISBN 0-8120-5510-1

PRINTED IN THE UNITED STATES OF AMERICA
3 4 5 6   620   9 8 7 6 5 4 3 2

CONTENTS

FOR SUSAN IMPERIALE AND KAREN LIPPERT

Thanks to the pasta tasters—
Bernie Kinzer, Steve Leskody, and Jack Burson.
Special thanks to John Imperiale
for some wine suggestions,
and very special thanks to Carole Berglie,
our extraordinary editor.

INTRODUCTION

*L*ife in Italy is spectacular! Italy is a country of dark green palms and blue-gray olive trees; the oleander blooms in multiple shades of pink. There are fields of deep red poppies, and the lantana on the countryside is eternal springtime. Stone houses—worn gray and filled with history—are silhouetted by trees bent to suit the wind. In kitchens, pantries, and shops are strings of red-hot dried peppers. And wherever there is a family, one sees the eight-quart vessel filled with boiling, double-boiling water waiting to receive the homemade pasta.

In the markets are the glowing colors and full-flavored aromas that immediately inspire the cook to set a creative menu. Bags of almonds and hazelnuts are for sale everywhere. Herbs from warm valleys and cool mountain slopes share their scents with those of the marvelous cheeses hanging over the doors and windows of the many small shops. Pasta is sold in endless shapes and forms. Garlic-filled sausages and dark smoked hams give the air a pungent, pleasing, and unmistakably spicy aroma. Fresh vegetables, usually only a few hours since harvest, adorn the creaky wooden stalls in designs as grand as the Baroque Italian churches.

No one denies that Italian cuisine is among the richest and most imaginative in the world. Why shouldn't it be? The same high-spirited flair for improvisation we find in the Italian arts surely is in their cuisine also. The Italian begins to cook in the market, selecting the freshest ingredients for the meal that will be a triumph of colors and flavors.

Italian food is beautiful as well as delicious. Combining tomato sauce and pimentos to create an opulent scarlet-colored dish is an uncanny Italian seventh sense. They combine egg and spinach pasta in *paglia e fieno* (straw and hay). Italians love color; look at the beautiful spinach gnocchi in Tuscany or the lasagna verde in Bologna. Color is alive in Venice; taste its risotto with green peas. Everywhere in Italy, salads are so green and verdant, tomatoes so red, provolones such a pale yellow. Putting them all together, as one sees all the time in Italy, creates the colorful Italian canvas.

Italians are also liberal with the raw materials for their food. Butter, cheese, oil, the best cuts of meat, chicken and turkey breasts, eggs, chicken and meat broth, raw and cooked hams are all freely used, but with an awareness of what good quality does for cooking. Italians insist on fresh foods, and in most Italian households the marketing is done twice a day. Everything is freshly cooked for each meal. Who needs fumets of fish, the *fonds de cuisine,* the meat glazes of the French? If the Italian cook cannot get the fresh product, he or she will bypass the dish and make something else.

This quality and freshness in food can be seen best in the pasta preparations. As children, we didn't know pasta could be bought in grocery stores. In our home, the wooden pole used for "hanging" pasta was a permanent piece of furniture, as was the family pasta-making board. Sometimes in addition to or in place of the wooden pole there were kitchen towels and white tablecloths dusted with flour, covering every inch of space one could find to hold the homemade fettuccine, cappelletti, tagliatelle, ravioli, and lasagne. The family pasta board, like the family cleaver which beheaded many live fowl, was a tool which received loving care and special security. It was about four feet square, thick and heavy, and never washed! Almost on a daily basis, sheets and sheets of pasta were made, rolled, and cut into many shapes and sizes.

Neighbors and relatives compared and discussed pasta and pasta boards with as much interest and concern as spring and fall fashions, new car models, or the World Series.

The foods of Italy are so very different from one area to the next, a reflection of the great diversity of the Italian countryside and the wealth of the land. The cooking of Milan contrasts with that of Venice. Both are markedly different from that of Umbria, Tuscany, and the coast of Liguria. Rome has her own specialties as do Genoa and Naples. And the kitchen aromas in Sardinia are decidedly different from those in Sicily. Each province in Italy retains its traditional versions. Ravioli may be laden with tomato sauce in one area but not in another. Yet even the names differ. The ravioli in one province may be called tortellini in another, anolini somewhere else, tortelli in yet another province, or even cappelletti, and agnolotti in still other provinces. Noodles, for example, have a thousand names: tagliarini, talitini, fettuccine, pappardelle; in Genoa they are trenetti and in Rome, tonnarelli. Pasta is different in Bari, Naples, Rome, Florence, Bologna, Venice, and Milan. But it is this very reason of unique cultural regional differences which makes pasta a glorious and infinitely interesting food.

Pasta is antiquity itself and its origins are not well known. Let's not try to fight the battle here of whether Marco Polo brought it to Italy because we believe he didn't. According to food writer Elizabeth David, *macarono* was made from *spelta* (small brown wheat) and first made its appearance in the reign of the magnanimous Prince Teodoric in Ravenna. By the end of the eighteenth century, pasta was deeply rooted in the tastes of the Italian populace. Some Italians in the north think that pasta as a daily food is unsuitable, but the fact remains that the majority of Italians, in spite of the various rice and polenta dishes in the north, continue to eat *pasta asciutta* at mid-day and probably some kind of pasta *in brodo* at night.

Pasta is what this book is all about. The basic, simple, and classic pasta recipes are presented here but Italians keep extending their repertoire by trying new combinations. For example, uncooked tomato sauces are popular in Italy today, and molded and stuffed pastas now occupy center stage on buffet lunches and supper tables. We've featured these, as well as a sampling of pastas in different colors. Pasta is a dish of great simplicity and popularity. Although its roots are foreign, it has also become an essential part of American cuisine. The Italian kitchen is an abundant and resourceful one, and out of it has come a style of cooking that is exuberant and colorful. The water is at a full and rolling boil. Let's make pasta.

EQUIPMENT AND INGREDIENTS

*M*ost pasta dishes probably can be made with the equipment and ingredients you have in your kitchen. However, procedures can be made easier, time can be saved, and your overall skills improved if you have the items described below.

EQUIPMENT

CHEESE GRATER: The traditional Italian type comes as a cylinder with a grater forming the lid; as you grate, the cheese falls inside the container. There are other types, however, that work equally well.

COLANDER: Absolutely indispensable in cooking pasta. Get a good stainless-steel one, large enough to hold 2 or more pounds of pasta.

DRYING POLE OR RACK: A 2-inch-thick wooden pole, about 6 feet long, dries pasta nicely; so does a small, folding pasta rack.

DOUGH SCRAPER: Use this a stainless-steel square with a wooden handle. Use it to bring together the various elements of the dough to form a ball.

FOOD CHOPPERS: In almost every Italian home you will find the *lunetta* or the *mezzaluna,* a crescent-shaped, 2-handled chopper. It chops garlic and parsley together. There are 1-bladed choppers and they work well, too.

FOOD MILL: This is invaluable in puréeing tomatoes, as it keeps the seeds separate and saves many hours of work. It is important to have the medium or large size and, although the stainless-steel type is more expensive, it is worth having, as it lasts a lifetime and will not corrode. Electric mixers, blenders, and food processors are not good for puréeing tomatoes because they macerate the seeds and integrate them into the purée rather than separate them from it.

PASTRY BOARD: It is important in making pasta to have a large, wooden pastry board. It should be at least 2 feet square, preferably larger. There are new types of pastry boards which are made of plastic and they are satisfactory for rolling out pasta. They don't look as "homey" as the old wooden ones, but the pasta does not stick to them and they are easy to clean. Also, they do not crack. The pasta board our family used as we grew up was never washed; it was always scraped and wiped with a cloth.

PASTA MACHINE: This is an important piece of equipment in any kitchen in which pasta is made. See page 193 for more information.

PASTA WHEELS: You should have a straight-edged one for cutting tortellini and other pasta and a fluted one for ravioli and pappardelle noodles.

RAVIOLI FORMS: Many pasta-makers prefer to use ravioli forms, however we think it is easier to roll out a strip of dough, put teaspoonfuls of filling on the dough, fold the dough in half, and use the ravioli cutter to shape them. The ones made in this way are never as uniform as those made in the form, but for our taste they are more interesting.

ROLLING PIN: The best rolling pins are made of hard, close-grained wood with a smooth finish. Wood rolls better than glass or ceramic and, also, does not break. The ideal rolling pin is approximately 1½ inches in diameter about 32 inches long. If you have a new one, wash it with soap and water, dry it well, give it a light coat of olive oil, wipe it down with a kitchen towel to absorb any excess oil, and then rub a little bit of all-purpose flour over the pin. Do this several times before using and you will have a rolling pin that will give you years of great satisfaction.

WOODEN FORKS AND SPOONS: Have many of these of differing lengths. When certain foods are sautéed, a long-handled spoon or fork is handy. A slotted spoon is handy in retrieving food from any cooking fat. Different sizes are good for stirring different amounts of pasta. Use wooden spoons and forks to stir pasta as it is cooking.

INGREDIENTS

It is important in all cooking to understand the nature of the ingredients that you put into a dish. Here we describe some of the ingredients that appear in pasta dishes in this book; the chapters on cheese and meats also include descriptions of types of cheeses and types of Italian meats, respectively.

ANCHOVIES: The anchovy is a dark blue and silver fish found in warm waters. Quite often, lesser members of the herring family such as sprats and pilchards are labelled anchovies and, although well spiced, pickled, or salted, are not the real thing. Anchovies average between 2½ and 3 inches, and are sold fresh or canned. The fresh fish is excellent, with white flesh and good flavor, but it is nothing like the taste of the cured fish. Plain salted anchovies should be soaked in water for about 30 minutes to remove some of their salt. With anchovies canned in oil, removing the salt is more difficult, so they should always be used with care unless the salty flavor is intended as a dominant part of the dish. A jar of salted anchovies will keep almost indefinitely provided they remain covered by liquid and are always taken out with a clean spoon. The canned, oiled anchovies also last well, again if covered in oil. Two brands which are commendable: Castle Village (from Morocco), imported by the A & A Food Product Corporation, Carlstadt, New Jersey, 07072; and Filetti di Alici, a Margiotta and Recca Brand, packed in Sciacca, Italy.

BUTTER: For eating and for much of our cooking, butter has no equal, both for flavor and for its enriching qualities. A simple melted butter sauce instantly elevates an equally simple dish. An excellent butter, salted or unsalted: Land O' Lakes, Arden Hills, Minnesota.

CHEESES: See pages 71–75.

GARLIC: Garlic is a must in our kitchen and has to be in yours. To crush garlic, sprinkle salt on the peeled clove and crush with the broad side of a large knife; or, without using salt, crush the garlic with the blunt top side of the knife; or put an unpeeled garlic clove on a flat surface and pound lightly with the back of your fist—the clove should split slightly, making it quite easy to remove the skin. To remove the odor of garlic (or onion) from a wooden cutting board or spoon, rub the surface with lemon juice.

HERBS: While fresh herbs are always preferable to dried, it is not always possible to grow them or find them in the markets. There is nothing wrong with using commercially dried herbs, but remember that they are stronger than fresh herbs; that when you substitute dried for fresh use ½ teaspoon (or ¼ teaspoon powdered) for every tablespoon of the fresh; that the flavor of dried herbs is intensified by crushing or rubbing them between your fingers; and that dried herbs should be replaced at least once a year. (Buy your herbs and spices in small packages to avoid waste.) Herbs should be kept in airtight containers in a dark and cool place.

Basil is a lovely aromatic herb with a spicy and aromatic scent. In Italy, basil leaves are best known in pesto, but it is also used to flavor tomato sauces, salads, and soups. Many say that basil is the most important herb in Italian cooking; we are apt to agree. The purists say that basil leaves should be torn apart in order to preserve the flavor, however we find that snipping them with scissors, especially when 4, 6, or 8 leaves are stacked together, doesn't destroy any flavor and is one of the easiest kitchen chores. We do the snipping right over the pasta, or into the tomato sauce, or onto the fresh tomato slices, and so on. Fresh basil is, of course, the best thing to use; it is very easy to grow. But there will be times when fresh basil is not available, so in those times, use dried basil. You cannot use dried basil in making pesto (please, don't even try), but it is very good in soups, salads, and tomato sauces.

Dill has many culinary uses. It has an almost identical threadlike foliage with fennel, and in taste too, although fennel is a much taller plant. Dill is combined beautifully with lamb, anchovies, salmon, chicken, or veal. Fennel is used both as a flavoring agent and as a vegetable. In our family, we couldn't live without fennel seed because it is a basic ingredient in our homemade pork sausage. Small packages of fennel seed come to us from Italy several times a year.

Oregano can be used in many ways but it must be remembered that its flavor is stronger, therefore discretion is urged.

Parsley comes in two ways: curly and flat. The latter is often referred to as Italian parsley, and many cooks feel that it is superior for taste while the curly parsley is better for garnishes. Try to use fresh parsley; the dried just doesn't measure up. It also freezes beautifully and will keep for months.

Rosemary is the herb of remembrance. It is obviously best fresh, but can be used dried with good results.

Sage is an herb used in Italy especially with liver and veal. It has a very distinct flavor.

NUTMEG: The hard, dark aromatic kernel of the fruit of the nutmeg tree is encased in a lacy covering, or aril, known as mace, which has the same flavor. The nutmeg "seed" and its lace covering are surely one of the world's wonders. Nutmeg is a pungent spice which should be used with discretion, grated straight onto the dish in which it is required. It can be used in both sweet and savory dishes and often flavors hot punches and other warming drinks.

OLIVE OIL: A common ingredient in Italian cooking and you'll find it, often along with butter, in many pasta recipes. Olive oil does not burn as fast as butter, and it is good to keep this in mind when you're preparing sauces or pasta dishes which take a long cooking time. Vegetable oil is not recommended as a substitute except for deep-frying.

We find the French oils too refined and suggest instead the Italian Berio and Progresso brands. Pastene is also good. Berio is lighter (thinner) than the other two, and we use it all the time; it is produced and bottled (or canned) in Lucca, Italy. One other excellent imported olive oil is Badia a Coltibuono Olio d'Uliva (olive oil extra virgin), produced and bottled by Tenuta di Coltibuono, s.r.l. Gaiole in Chianti (SI) Italy.

ONIONS: Like garlic, onions are used a lot in Italian cookery. To remove the odor of onion from wooden cutting tops, rub the surface with lemon juice. Onion tears are reduced if the onion is very cold before it is chopped; put the onion in the freezer for a half hour before chopping. Peeling under cold, running water also helps prevent tearing.

PASTA: Commercial brands of pasta vary in quality, but the best are made from hard wheat and eggs of good quality. We think the commercial pasta in the U.S. is good, probably because it is manufactured by Americans of Italian ancestry (Ronzoni, Buitoni, and so on), but the best commercial pasta is imported from Italy. The 2 best are the pastas of Pastificio del Verde—Fara San Martino—and Menucci. Other fine pastas from Italy are Spiga, La Molisana, and F.lli de Cecco di Filippo. These are from first-quality semolina and come in many shapes. They are obtainable in specialty stores and pasta shops.

TOMATOES: It is important to use the correct tomato for these pasta dishes. Even when a recipe calls for canned tomatoes, which is quite often since their particular qualities are appreciated, use Italian canned plum tomatoes. Only then will the true flavor of the dish be there. Both the Pope and Vitelli brands of imported San Marzano plum tomatoes are excellent. Three other good imported Italian brands are Antonio Contorno and D. Coluccio, and Tana, packed for Antonio Piccini and Sons. A good domestic brand is Asti. When using fresh tomatoes, choose firm ripe ones. Never ripen fresh tomatoes in direct sunlight; instead place them in a brown paper bag and leave the bag in indirect sunlight. To remove tomato skins, dunk the tomatoes in boiling water for 10 seconds, then dip them in cold water for 10 seconds. With a paring knife, remove the stem and peel the skin off. When you need puréed tomatoes, run them through a food mill to separate the seeds and skin; do not use a food processor or blender for this.

VINEGARS: Vinegars, as a rule, won't count too much in pasta cookery except when it comes to some cool salads. But it is so important to so much Italian cookery that 2 brands should be mentioned: Balsamic Vinegar of Modena; and a red wine vinegar by Badia a Coltibuono.

HOW TO MAKE AND COOK PASTA
HOW TO SAUCE AND EAT IT

*B*asically there are 2 kinds of pasta: the homemade pasta—*pasta fatta in casa*—and the factory mass-produced kind. In this country, the factory-made pasta has been the most popular, and it is only recently that pasta shops have opened making fresh pasta daily.

On some packages of factory-made pasta you will see the words *pasta di pura semola di grano duro;* this means that the pasta is made from the fine flour obtained from the cleaned endosperm or heart of the durum (hard) wheat grain. This is the cream of wheat, and you should select these brands. (We have found excellent brands of factory-made pasta; see page 7.) In Italy some factory-produced pastas are made with eggs. There the rule is that the best pasta has 5 eggs to each kilo of pasta, although much pasta produced in Italy and surely also in this country is made without eggs. It is important to remember that as far as the difference is concerned, other than taste, factory-made pasta takes as much as 15 minutes to cook. Freshly made pasta takes about 5 minutes or less.

One problem with Italian cooks is that they never measure ingredients. Classic examples were our mother and grandmother. It was impossible to sit either of them down to measure their formulas for pasta. In spite of this, everything they ever made was totally delicious. Another problem with pasta recipes is that flour differs as do eggs. Flour varies in its quality to absorb liquids; eggs vary in size. Since pasta is basically a combination of flour and eggs, it is difficult to be totally exacting in the amounts needed for perfect pasta. The basic rule is that for every egg, use ¾ cup of flour. If you use 1 egg, use ¾ cup all-purpose flour; 1½ cups for 2 eggs; 2¼ cups for 3 eggs; 3 cups for 4 eggs, and so on. It

is not difficult to make pasta; you simply have to develop a feel for it. Use these guidelines, try it, and if it can take a little more flour, add it. You will get to know the feel. Once you roll out the dough, cook it, drain it, and taste it, you will know if you have used the right proportion of ingredients.

Pasta is made differently all over Italy. In some places, no water is added; in other parts of Italy some water is used. In yet others, just some drops of oil are used. We suggest a combination of eggs, all-purpose flour, some salt, some olive oil, and some lukewarm water. This combination works best with American flours. For all pastas to be cut as tagliatelle, fettuccine, pappardelle, maltagliati, cannelloni, or manicotti, use the ingredients given in the basic recipe. For all pastas to be filled and sealed (such as cappelletti, tortellini, or ravioli), substitute milk for water to improve the seal.

One-Egg Pasta

(2 servings,
about ½ pound)

3/4 cup all-purpose flour
1 egg
1/4 teaspoon salt
1/2 tablespoon olive oil
1/4 tablespoon lukewarm water
   or milk

Two-Egg Pasta

(3 to 4 servings,
about ¾ pound)

1½ cups all-purpose flour
2 eggs
1/2 teaspoon salt
3/4 tablespoon olive oil
3/4 tablespoon lukewarm water
   or milk

Three-Egg Pasta

(5 to 6 servings,
about 1 pound)

2¼ cups all-purpose flour
3 eggs
3/4 teaspoon salt
1 tablespoon olive oil
1 tablespoon lukewarm water
   or milk

Four-Egg Pasta

(7 to 8 servings,
about 1½ pounds)

3 cups all-purpose flour
4 eggs
1 teaspoon salt
1½ tablespoons olive oil
1 tablespoon lukewarm water
   or milk

On the preceding pages: Spaghetti with Pesto Sauce (recipe on page 44); Filled Lasagne Rolls with Two Sauces (recipe on page 164).

Measure level cup and part-cup quantities of flour according to the quantity of pasta you wish to make. Put the flour on a flat surface or in a bowl and form a well deep enough to hold the egg(s). Keep the sides high enough to prevent the egg(s) from running out.

Break the egg(s) into the well. Add other ingredients. (If you are making pasta to stuff, add milk instead of water.) With a small wooden fork or a whisk, beat the egg(s) lightly and, in so doing, begin to pick up a little of the flour from inside the well with the fork or whisk. Incorporate the flour into the egg(s) until no longer runny. The mixture will begin to look like paste. A good technique for integrating the flour with the egg(s) is to whisk with one hand and, with the other, hold or support the outside wall of the well. By pushing the outer edge of the flour wall with your hand, some of the flour will fall into the well. If the dough is sticky, add a little more flour.

With your hands, bring all the flour from the outside of the well toward the center and make a ball with the dough. After some mixing, the dough will be soft. If still sticky, pick it up between your hands and mix further. Set ball aside and, with a knife or pastry scraper, scrape up all the crumbs of flour which caked on the working surface. Also remove the caked flour from your hands. These scraps can be incorporated with the rest of the dough, but we think it is better to discard them and use a little fresh flour in the kneading process.

Put the ball of dough on a flat surface and, with the heel of your hand, push down firmly into the center. Give the dough a slight turn, and push down again. Dust your hands with flour as the dough is likely to stick in the beginning, but in any case keep kneading. A 1-egg recipe generally requires 5 minutes of kneading; a 2-egg recipe will require 7 minutes, and so on increasing in length with the increase in quantity of ingredients. The dough should be smooth and satiny and not tough. Once the dough is kneaded into a smooth ball, cover it with a bowl or tea towel and let rest for about 15 minutes. If you have made a large batch of dough, then divide it in smaller pieces, so each piece is no larger than that for a 2-egg pasta. Your pieces of dough should be only as large as you have room to roll them out.

ROLLING OUT THE DOUGH BY HAND

Dust a clean surface lightly with flour. Put a ball of dough on the surface and, with a rolling pin, begin to flatten it by rolling forward first and then backward away from you. With each roll, rotate the dough one quarter turn. In this way, it opens out into a regular circle. Try to keep the dough as round as possible and keep rolling it away from you without putting too much weight on it. You should have a sheet of pasta that is approximately ⅛th inch thick.

When we were kids we used to watch our grandmother curl the far end of the pasta sheet around the end of a rolling pin and roll it toward her. Some people curl the near end of the pasta sheet and roll away from them. Whichever direction, curling the pasta around the pin stretches the dough to the desired thinness. If the dough becomes a bit sticky, flour it lightly and roll out the sheet. Use as little flour as possible, however, and move quickly because pasta dries out fast. If you work at it and stay with it, you'll have no trouble. The pasta should be transparent and thin so that it doesn't feel any heavier than several layers of tissue paper. In other words, it should be very light to the feel and almost as if you can look through it.

To make fettuccine or any of the string pastas, roll up the pasta sheet as you would a jelly roll. Roll it tightly so it can be handled and cut easily. Hold the roll with one hand and with the other, slice to the thickness you desire. When the sheet of pasta is sliced, open out the noodles with both hands and put them on a lightly floured towel to dry for several minutes. In place of flour, cornmeal may be used and, after you've tried both, you may end up preferring the cornmeal. It's fun undoing the cut pasta rolls. Grab several with both hands, raise your hands as if to release the pasta, but don't release. Shake out the pasta strips, your hands still clinging to them, and set them gently on the towel.

USING A PASTA MACHINE

Pasta machines are fitted with smooth rollers that will produce several thicknesses of sheet (which is what pasta dough is called when it has been rolled out, whether by hand or by machine). A knob can be turned to widen or narrow the opening between the smooth rollers. (Our machine has 6 settings.) Cutting rollers, which can be attached to the machine, slice the sheet to the noodle width of your desire. Pasta machines are usually fitted with 2-mm and 6-mm cutting rollers. (The 2 cutting rollers are attached to the machine in a single piece.) Additional rollers of 1.5-mm, 4-mm, and 12-mm width are also available. Only 1 pasta width may be cut at a time.

Run each ball of dough through the opening 2 times *without* folding. It is not necessary to fold the dough in 2 or 3 layers when putting the pasta through the rollers for a second or third time. When this is done—that is, folding over—the pasta rolls out of shape.

It is not necessary to put rolled-out dough pieces through each opening. Skip every other one. For example, on a 6-notch machine, roll dough through openings 6 (the thickest), 4, 2, and 1 (the thinnest).

Very lightly flour each strip of dough after it is rolled. Once the dough is sprinkled with flour, rub the palm of your hand up or down the strip to lightly cover it with flour.

The dough ball from a 4-egg pasta recipe should be cut into 10 or 12 pieces before rolling out. Larger dough balls (5- and 6-egg recipes) will require cutting into more pieces; smaller dough balls (2- and 3-egg recipes) will require fewer.

For information on specific pasta machines, see pages 193–195.

CUTTING THE PASTA

The catalogue of 1 Italian pasta manufacturer shows over 200 pasta types. Although most of these have to be machine made, you can make about 20 different varieties at home. Here are brief descriptions of some of the most popular and how to cut them.

TAGLIATELLE: These are the most common form of homemade pasta, known in Rome as *fettuccine*. The pasta is rolled up and cut into ¼-inch widths. (The Italian Academy of Cooking says they must be slightly less than ¼ inch.) The fettuccine eaten in Rome are a little thicker and a little less wide than the classic tagliatelle. (See drawing 1.)

TAGLIARINI: Also called *taliolini,* these are extremely thin noodles, about ¹⁄₁₆th inch wide. They are excellent in soups, especially chicken and meat broths. (See drawing 1.)

1

CAPELLINI: Also known as *capelli d'angelo* (angel's hair), these are a thinner version of tagliarini. It's easy to cut tagliarini on a pasta machine or by hand, but capellini are so thin they have to be bought in a pasta shop, grocery store, or supermarket.

PAPPARDELLE: About ⅝ths inch wide, these are cut with a fluted ravioli wheel. Once the pasta sheet is rolled out, cut directly on the flat surface. Easy and fun to cut. (See drawing 2.)

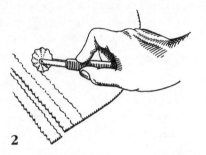

2

MALTAGLIATI: This means "bad cut" (*mal* = bad, *tagliati* = cut). We can't explain the nature of the Italian who cuts daily straight lines of tagliatelle, fettuccine, or lasagne and then gets bored and wants to cut badly, but we like the idea and the resultant pasta. It is so good in so many ways, especially in thicker soups where chick peas or beans play a dominant role. Once the pasta sheet is rolled up, the cut is made at an angle, cutting off 1 triangular piece of dough on the near side of the roll. One cut on the far side and then a straight cut produce a third triangle. (See drawing 3.)

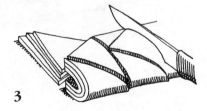

3

QUADRUCCI: Or *quadrettini,* these are little squares of pasta. First cut pasta into tagliatelle shape, then cut crosswise to make little squares. (See drawing 4.)

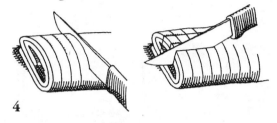

4

CANNELLONI: These are similar to manicotti squares. Once the pasta sheet is rolled out, cut the pasta into rectangles 3 × 4 inches. It is best to make these with a pasta machine such as our Rollecta. Roll out wide strips of dough, as thin as possible and cut into rectangles 3 × 4 inches. (See drawing 5.)

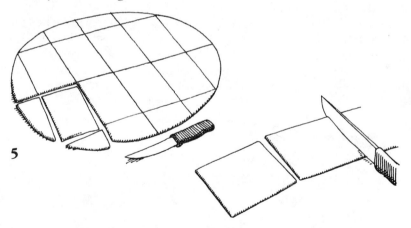

5

CAPPELLETTI: Cut 1½-inch squares from a pasta sheet. Each square receives about ¼ teaspoon of a filling and is folded over, almost diagonally but not quite. The edges are pressed to secure the filling and a cappelletto is bent around a finger, almost always the index finger, and one point is pressed over the other.

TORTELLINI: Similar to cappelletti but made of 2-inch-round pasta pieces. They are filled, folded over and sealed as are cappelletti. (See drawing 6.)

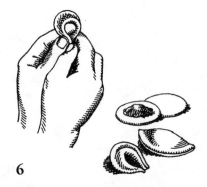

6

TORTELLONI: A kind of ravioli, cut directly from the pasta sheet. Trim the sheet away from you to make a straight edge—but use a fluted ravioli wheel. Place about ½ teaspoon of filling 1½ inches apart in a straight line, approximately 2 inches from the straight edge. Pick up the edge and fold it over (toward you); this fold covers the many little hills of filling. With the fluted wheel, cut the filled strip away from the pasta sheet and then cut between each mound. (See drawing 7.)

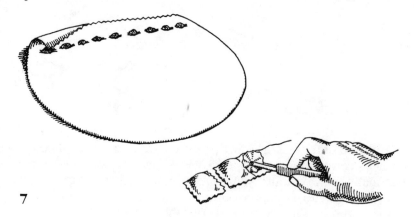

7

RAVIOLI: Trim and straighten the edges of a pasta sheet with a fluted wheel. Place a level teaspoon of ravioli filling 1½ inches apart across the surface of the pasta, in checkerboard style. Use a very thin pastry brush (or your index finger) dipped in water and draw lines along and across the mounds of filling. Carefully lift up another pasta sheet and lay it over the first. Run your index finger along and across the fillings again sealing the top layer to the bottom where the water was outlined. With a fluted wheel, cut along and across the mounds of filling, cutting them into 1½-inch squares. Once cut, transfer the ravioli squares to a floured cookie sheet or towel. Cook the ravioli as soon as you can, but if they must wait before cooking, cover them with a lightly dampened towel. If longer than 1 or 2 hours, cover with plastic wrap and set in refrigerator or freeze. (In place of tablespoons of filling, you can put the filling in a pastry bag fitted with a No. 5 or 6 pastry tube.)

Another method is that, instead of covering with a whole pasta sheet, cut sheet into 3-inch strips after straightening edges of pasta circle. Set fillings on one side of strip, 1½ inches apart and 1 inch from a side of the strip, folding over the other strip. Seal with water as in method #1 and cut along all 4 edges of each square with a fluted wheel. These ravioli must be cut along *4* sides. Reserve or freeze as in method #1.

A third method, if using the Rollecta type pasta machine, is to roll out pasta strips 3 inches wide and follow steps as in method #1. Yet another method is to use a pasta machine to roll out the dough and then use a ravioli form to cut and seal. The form is in 2 parts, a bottom and a top. Cut the pasta sheet so it is larger (longer *and* wider) than the form. Use the form itself as a guide by placing on top of dough and then cutting to size. You will need 2 sheets of dough, 1 for the bottom and 1 for the top. Flour the bottom sheet adequately so it doesn't stick to the form. Lay the first sheet on the form and press down with the top part of the form to make pouches to hold the filling. Remove the top part of the form and fill the pouches. (Use a spoon, fork, or pastry bag.) Place another sheet of dough on top of the filling and press down with your fingertips and remove air pockets. The top pasta sheet should be flat and somewhat even to the top of the form. Then roll the rolling pin over the form until the ravioli square shapes are visible; they are like small jagged teeth and most forms are designed to make 12 ravioli. Turn out the ravioli and if any adhere to the form, push a little to release them. There is available an individual ravioli form, a square with ragged teeth; it works but it seems a nuisance to "stamp" out each ravioli when other methods and forms are so easy to handle.)

BUTTERFLIES (FARFALLE) or (STRICHETTI): Use your fluted pastry wheel and cut along each edge of a rectangular sheet of dough to serate it with the pastry wheel cutter; divide the sheet into rectangles (use a ruler to start with) 2 inches long, and 1 inch wide. Pinch the center of each rectangle to form butterflies. (See drawing 8.)

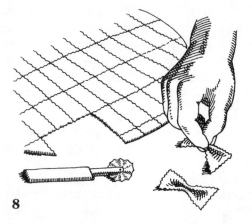

8

MANICOTTI: Traditionally these are cut from hand-rolled pasta sheets or from pasta strips rolled through a manual or electric pasta machine. The size is 4 by 4 inches square and the pasta should be as thin as possible. A nonclassic, but excellent alternative procedure is to use crespelle (page 24).

LASAGNE: These are cut into long strips from a pasta sheet or are made from a manual or electric pasta machine. If you don't have the extra cutting attachment for lasagne, just put the dough through the rollers and after you have the thickness you want, cut the dough strip into lasagne pieces. Lasagne may be cut 2 or 3 inches wide, and 9 to 12 inches long. The size of the strip is somewhat dependent on the size of the baking dish you will use. To cut lasagne strips, use a plain or fluted wheel, or a sharp knife.

COOKING THE PASTA

It is difficult to understand why there should be so much mystery surrounding the cooking of pasta. Actually it is one of the simplest things to do if one follows some very simple rules.

Use a large cooking vessel and a lot of water. Generally, allow 4 quarts of water to 1 pound of pasta. Heat the water over high heat and bring it to a rolling boil. Have the water boil for several minutes before you put in the pasta. Add 1 tablespoon oil as the water approaches a boil. Many cooks omit the oil, but we believe that it separates the strands of pasta. It also helps keep the cooking water from boiling over.

When the water is at a rolling boil, add approximately 1½ tablespoons of salt for every 4 quarts of water. Put the pasta in the water *all at once.* As soon as the pasta is in the water, and sometimes long strands of pasta will take a little time to become fully immersed in the water, stir immediately and frequently with a wooden fork. You will see the strands of pasta separating as each strand surrounds itself with water. When fully separated, you can stop stirring continuously, but do so every minute or so. (We believe it a cardinal sin to cut any spaghetti or other long pasta in half; you should learn to handle the full strands.)

When several minutes have gone by, remove a strand with a wooden fork and test. *Al dente* means "firm to the bite," and that is how Italians eat pasta. Remember that even in the draining process, the water is so hot that once the pot is removed from the stove, the pasta is still cooking. Even while saucing it with hot olive oil or a tomato sauce, the pasta is still cooking.

Do not run the pasta under cold water. Put it into a colander, shake the colander to remove as much liquid as possible, and return it to the pan in which it cooked. At 1 or 2 tablespoons of butter (sometimes specified in the recipe), then toss lightly and sauce it. Overcooking pasta destroys its texture, so be sure that it is *al dente*.

All store-bought pasta comes with directions on the box but they are not always reliable. Rely instead upon yourself, and test the pasta as it cooks.

Note that we suggest you drain the pasta and then return it to the pot in which it cooked so as to coat it briefly with butter. The best way to toss the pasta is simply by stirring with 2 wooden forks or spoons, mixing and tossing the pasta. Lift and stir. Often it is best to add half your sauce while the pasta is in the pot, toss again, and then transfer the pasta to the serving plates. Before taking it to the table, add the remaining sauce and whatever cheese or garnish is called for in the recipe. Many of the recipes call for adding more cheese when serving the pasta, and this should be on the side.

One of our favorite sayings is that "pasta waits for no one." As soon as it is cooked, drained, and sauced, serve it.

HOW TO EAT PASTA

Some people think the U.S. has been "pasta-rized." They may be correct when one thinks of the enthusiasm for farfalle, fettuccine, and fusilli. Since spaghetti is at an all-time high, how should one eat it? Do you sprinkle cheese on pasta with seafood sauce? How about bread with pasta? What is the best cheese?

Emily Post says to twirl spaghetti against a spoon with the tips of a fork resting against the curve of the plate. Every expert we know says no to the use of a fork and spoon. Our grandparents spent hours teaching us how to eat pasta without using a spoon, how to twirl our forks so that not a strand of spaghetti would be hanging down as we lifted them to our mouths. But they said it was okay to allow a few strands of pasta to hang down. If the pasta is cooked *al dente,* they would explain, a few strands will hang. When the pasta twirls too neatly and fully around the fork, it probably is overcooked. The one time to use a spoon is if the sauce is very liquid—a clam sauce, for example; you'd need the spoon to eat the remaining sauce once the pasta is gone, or you might use the spoon just to prevent splattering.

It is correct to place a spoon at each place setting, however. In Italy it is customary to first place the pasta in a bowl or on a plate. Then the sauce is spooned over and finally cheese is sprinkled on top. The fork and spoon are used to toss the pasta with the sauce and cheese; then you eat the pasta with your fork alone.

Here is how to use a fork. Put the fork into a few strands of spaghetti. Let the tines of the fork rest against the curve of the bowl or the curved indentation of the plate, and twirl the fork around giving it brief, quick lifts to prevent too much pasta from accumulating.

There isn't much agreement about bread with pasta. Some will say no, but others serve bread. After all, it is always on the table at restaurants. We believe that when at home, you need the bread to dip in the left-over sauce once the pasta is eaten. If the sauce is good for pasta, it is good for bread too.

Imported parmesan reggiano, at least 2 years old before it is exported, is probably the best cheese for pasta, although pecorino goes especially well with some sauces. But cheese with seafood pasta is generally avoided, although you might consider adding freshly grated parmesan to shrimp and squid with spaghettini. In the last analysis, it is all a matter of taste.

HIGH-PROTEIN PASTAS

These pastas are made with whole-wheat, soy, or jerusalem artichoke flours fortified with natural protein and wheat gluten. The manufacturers claim considerably more protein in these products than there is in regular pasta (as much as 70 percent more). They further emphasize their natural ingredients and no artificial enrichment.

As a rule, no preservatives or chemicals are added to these products, nor is salt. The jerusalem artichoke is 100 percent nonstarch; tubers are dehydrated into an artichoke powder which retains all its natural ingredients.

High-protein pastas come in all sizes and shapes, are much darker in color, take a little longer to cook, and may be sauced, baked, or filled as are homemade and regular store-bought pastas.

OTHER PASTAS

When you hear the word *pasta,* you might automatically think of fettuccine or ravioli, but there are other pastas that could be considered. We offer here 2 recipes: one for gnocchi, small dumplings usually made with flour or potato, eggs, butter, and seasonings; and crespelle, or manicotti shells, which you can use to stuff as you would the classic manicotti.

Potato Gnocchi

Gnocchi should be as well known in this country as are spaghetti and macaroni, but unfortunately they are not. They are popular in northern Italy, where they are made with cornmeal (polenta) or puréed potatoes. Plain gnocchi are served with chicken livers or some kind of rich meat or vegetable sauce; other times they are baked with butter and cheese.

1. Bake the potatoes in a preheated 350-degree oven for 1 hour. Peel and put them through a food mill or mash them.

2. In a large bowl, mix the egg yolks, salt, nutmeg, and grated cheese; mix well. Add the mashed potatoes, then add the flour, a little at a time, until a dough forms and holds together. The dough should be soft but firm enough to roll.

SERVES 3 TO 4

INGREDIENTS

5 Idaho potatoes
2 egg yolks, at room
   temperature
1/4 teaspoon salt
1/4 teaspoon grated nutmeg
1/2 cup grated parmesan
   cheese
1 1/2 cups all-purpose flour

3. On a floured board, roll small amounts of dough into small cylinders about 1½ inches in diameter; cut each cylinder into ½-inch pieces. Take each piece and press it (and roll it) against a cheese grater. This gives the gnocchi a nice design and texture.

4. Drop the gnocchi gently into 4 quarts of boiling salted water, and cook for 5 minutes. Drain, and top the gnocchi with the desired sauce.

Crespelle (Manicotti Pancakes)

1. Break the eggs into a bowl and beat with a whisk. Stir in the water. Add the flour gradually, stirring with the whisk. Add salt to taste, stir, and let stand for 30 minutes.

2. Heat a 7- or 8-inch crêpe pan or small nonstick skillet over moderate heat, and brush lightly with melted butter. Add about 3 tablespoons of batter, and tilt the pan this way and that until the batter covers the bottom. (The shells should be quite thin, but substantial enough to handle.) Cook about 30 seconds on one side, then turn the shell using a spatula or your hands and cook on the other side briefly (2 or 3 seconds). Slide the shell out of the pan.

MAKES 12 PANCAKES

INGREDIENTS
3 eggs
1 cup water
1 cup all-purpose flour
salt
melted butter

3. Repeat this process until all the batter is used, brushing the skillet lightly with butter if necessary before each shell is made.

NOTE
Shells or crêpes can be made 1 or 2 days in advance and refrigerated, or frozen and kept for weeks. Stack them on foil or freezer paper and wrap well. It is not necessary to interline each shell with paper.

On the following pages: Eggplant and Fresh Tagliatelle (recipe on page 90); Artichoke Hearts and Carrots with Spaghettini (recipe on page 87).

ESSENTIAL SAUCES

I talians say that pastas tend to taste alike, but they declare that each is given a life of its own when served with the proper sauce. No matter how exciting the stuffing and however well a particular pasta has been cooked, its ultimate success depends on the sauce with which it is served. The proper sauce for a certain pasta should be determined by the shape and, even more importantly, by the lightness or heaviness of the pasta itself.

Rigatoni, ziti, or small unfilled shells, *maruzzelle,* and other similar pasta should be served with a highly flavored sauce that can be savored through the thickness of the pasta and that is plentiful enough to fill the hollow of each shell or tube. A robust bolognese sauce, or *ragù bolognese,* would be good with such pastas because it has the character to stand up to the heavier pastas. But as glorious tasting as this is, a more delicate sauce is needed for string pastas such as vermicelli. When fresh basil and tomatoes are at their best, we make a sauce composed of the youngest of sliced scallions, fresh basil, Italian leaf parsley, and peeled, seeded and chopped fresh tomatoes—all lightly cooked in butter for only a few minutes. This simple sauce is at its best with buttered vermicelli or spaghettini.

Classic Italian sauces are easy to prepare (especially when compared to French sauces), have fewer pitfalls, and possess a freshness that many French sauces lack. In this chapter, we've included some essential sauces. You'll also find more sauces in other chapters of this book.

THE BUTTER SAUCES

Fettuccine is Roman; it is the Roman name for pasta made with eggs which elsewhere is called tagliatelle. In this country, they are called noodles. Whichever name is used, each is the recipient of the most basic and one of the best Italian pasta sauces—butter and cheese. There is no simpler sauce, and the pasta, combined with unsalted butter and freshly grated parmesan cheese, can't be surpassed. The basic butter sauce can be extended in a number of ways, but a classic method is to add pancetta or bacon, or—the ultimate—fresh white truffles.

THE OLIVE OIL SAUCES

Some sauces center on olive oil and garlic. These 2 ingredients make one of the best combinations, whether the garlic is raw or lightly sautéed. One of the more robust sauces is what the Italians call *all'aglio e olio,* or garlic and oil—a sauce made by lightly cooking lots of chopped garlic in olive oil and mixing it with the hot drained pasta.

The basic recipe, *aglio e olio,* is one of the most popular in the metropolitan centers of Italy and is fast becoming "the thing to do" in major U.S. cities. It is believed that pasta *aglio e olio* has restorative powers, and anyone having a night on the town spares the next morning's hangover if he or she has eaten a large bowl of this before going to bed.

THE TOMATO SAUCES

There are 3 tomato sauces fundamental to any pasta-cooking repertoire. They are easy to make, and they are also practical because they can be made ahead and frozen. The first sauce is a simple combination of butter and tomatoes flavored with onion and carrot. No garlic, no olive oil, no tomato paste, no long cooking; it is fresh and light, and may be considered the ultimate tomato sauce for anyone's taste. The second is also a fresh and delightful sauce, different from the first in that it has olive oil but no butter, and has more vegetables, which cook with the tomatoes first. Still no garlic, no tomato paste or purée, and no long cooking; the only herb is parsley, so this sauce is still a fresh, reasonably light sauce with lots of fresh flavor. The third sauce combines butter and olive oil with tomatoes. Unlike the second, the vegetables in the third are first sautéed in olive oil and butter for added flavor. Although the vegetables become well cooked, there is a crunchy texture to this sauce that doesn't exist in the others. These sauces are very alive with thin spaghetti; in fact, we cook them mostly with capellini (angel's hair), but they are delicious with any pasta, regardless of size.

One of the best known sauces, particularly in the U.S., is the neopolitan or marinara sauce. In Naples, it is prepared with fresh tomatoes, although marinara sauces in the U.S. are almost always prepared with canned tomatoes. But whether using canned or fresh tomatoes, the ideal marinara sauce should have a smooth texture and be lightly scented with olive oil, onions, and anchovies. Served over buttered hot pasta, a wine-dark marinara sauce makes the perfect dish. It also serves as a good base for many other sauces. *Spaghetti alle vongole* (spaghetti with clams and tomato sauce), so much beloved by the Romans, is made by cooking raw clams in a marinara sauce. When the clams open, their juices not only thin the sauce appropriately, but flavor it as well. Mushrooms, other shellfish, chicken, fish, or meat may also be cooked in a marinara sauce.

But this is only the beginning of tomato sauces. Included here are filetto sauce and *ragù bolognese,* a quick ragu, a tomato sauce with marsala and one with beef, and an uncooked tomato sauce.

OTHER SAUCES

Genoa is famous for many things, especially its pesto sauce. It is a classic and precise dish although over the years it has been a sauce of many substitutions and variations. For example, pinenuts and walnuts can be combined and even some almonds can be added.

Food processors and electric blenders make it easy now to prepare pesto. It just doesn't seem practical or even worthwhile these days to pound the garlic, oil, and pinenuts in a mortar the way you might get it in a Genoese household. But however you make the pesto, when it is thinned with a little pasta-cooking water and stirred into a bowl of hot buttered pasta, the fragrance and bright green color make this a memorable dish. It can be used with almost every type of pasta; it is distinctive without being overpowering and subtle without being bland.

Some sauces depend on anchovies; here we concentrate on 2 of them. The first amalgamates oil, garlic, anchovy fillets, and red pepper flakes; the second creates an anchovy sauce with capers and black olives for linguini.

The balsamella sauce of flour, butter, and milk is essential to many baked and stuffed pastas such as lasagne. We include one version used for other recipes in this book.

Butter, Cheese, and Cream Sauce

1. In a heavy heatproof casserole, combine the butter and ½ cup of the cream. Simmer over low heat until the butter has melted; this should take less than 1 minute. Turn off the heat.

2. Prepare pasta, drain, then transfer to the casserole with the butter and cream. Turn the heat on under the casserole and, with 2 wooden spoons or 2 wooden forks, lift the pasta and toss well, coating it completely with the sauce. Add the remaining ½ cup cream, parmesan cheese, some salt and pepper to taste, and nutmeg. Toss briefly for another minute, correct the seasoning, and serve immediately with more grated cheese on the side.

SERVES 4
for 1 pound pasta, preferably homemade fettuccine

INGREDIENTS
¼ pound butter
1 cup heavy cream
salt
1 cup freshly grated parmesan cheese, approximately
freshly ground black pepper
pinch of freshly grated nutmeg

NOTE
The basis for *Fettucine al Alfredo,* this sauce is best when made with homemade pasta. According to food historians, there really was a Roman restaurateur with the name Alfredo.

Butter, Cheese, and Garlic Sauce

1. Cream together the butter, garlic, and salt until the mixture is smooth.

2. When the pasta is cooked *al dente,* drain well and turn it into a warmed, buttered serving dish. Quickly mix in garlic butter and grated cheese. Serve in warmed dishes and sprinkle on pepper.

SERVES 4
for 1 pound spaghettini

INGREDIENTS
½ pound butter, at room
temperature
3 cloves garlic, very finely
minced
1 teaspoon salt
½ cup freshly grated
parmesan cheese
freshly ground black pepper

NOTE
About ¼ cup of finely chopped fresh herbs may be added to the garlic butter; parsley, scallion tops, or basil would be appropriate.

Butter, Cheese, and Bacon Sauce

1. In a heavy saucepan or skillet, melt the butter and cook the bacon until crisp. Grind in the pepper and blend well.

SERVES 4
for 1 pound spaghetti or thin spaghetti

INGREDIENTS
3 tablespoons butter
½ pound lean bacon, diced
freshly ground black pepper

2. Toss half the bacon mixture with the cooked, hot pasta; serve the remaining bacon on top. Sprinkle with cheese and add more pepper according to taste; the classic dish is very peppery.

NOTE
This sauce, a Roman specialty, comes from the Trastevera area which lies across the Tiber. If you've been in Rome, you've probably been there.

½ cup freshly grated romano or parmesan cheese

Butter, Cheese, and White Truffle Sauce

1. In a mixing bowl, cream the butter with a whisk until it is smooth and fluffy. Beat in ½ cup of cheese and then the cream, adding the cream about 1 tablespoon at a time and beating well after each addition.

2. Cook the pasta, drain it, and place it in a heated bowl. Add the butter-cheese sauce, salt to taste, and liberal grindings of black pepper. With 2 forks, toss the pasta until every strand is coated. Taste for seasoning; you may want more salt. Gently stir in the truffle slices or sprinkle them over the top and serve at once.

SERVES 4 TO 6
for 1 pound fettuccine or other thin pasta

INGREDIENTS
¼ pound butter, at room temperature
1 cup grated parmesan cheese
⅓ cup heavy cream
salt
freshly ground black pepper
1 white truffle, about 1" in diameter, sliced paper-thin

NOTE
If you plan to make the sauce ahead of time, cover and refrigerate it, but let it return to room temperature for about 1 hour before serving.

Butter and Egg Sauce

1. Cut the butter into small pieces and set aside.

2. Beat the eggs lightly in a small bowl. Add a pinch of salt and pepper, and set aside.

3. Cook the pasta *al dente*, drain thoroughly, and return to the pan in which it cooked. Add the butter pieces all at once, stirring to melt. Add the eggs and nutmeg and cook over very low heat, stirring constantly to coat each strand of pasta with sauce. Just when the egg is about to congeal—about 2 or 3 minutes—remove pot from the heat and serve pasta in warmed bowls. Add more freshly ground pepper to taste and serve with freshly grated cheese.

SERVES 4
for 1 pound fettuccine or other thin pasta

INGREDIENTS
3 tablespoons butter
3 eggs
salt
freshly ground black pepper
pinch of freshly ground nutmeg
1 cup freshly grated parmesan cheese

Olive Oil and Garlic Sauce

1. In a skillet heat the oil, add the garlic, and cook just until garlic begins to color. (If the garlic turns brown, you'll have to start over using fresh garlic and oil.)

2. Add the salt, pepper, and parsley. Stir well and remove from the heat immediately. This should take only several seconds; the salt, pepper, and parsley are not to be cooked, but rather they flavor the oil. Toss with pasta.

SERVES 4
for 1 pound spaghetti, spaghettini, vermicelli

INGREDIENTS
½ cup + 1 tablespoon olive oil

NOTE

Make this sauce while the pasta is cooking. Have the garlic and parsley ready to add to the skillet along with the other ingredients. As soon as the pasta is cooked, drain and sauce it. Add freshly grated parmesan to taste, if you wish.

4 cloves garlic, chopped fine
1½ teaspoons salt
freshly ground black pepper
4 tablespoons finely chopped
*   flat parsley*

Olive Oil and Broccoli Sauce

1. In a large skillet add the olive oil and the anchovies. Cook over medium heat until the anchovies combine with the oil, using a wooden spoon to dissolve the anchovy pieces.

2. Add the cooked broccoli florets and the pepper, and sauté over moderate heat for 5 minutes. Check and adjust salt seasoning if necessary.

SERVES 4
for 1 pound string pasta

INGREDIENTS
½ cup olive oil
6 flat anchovy filets, chopped
*   coarse*
½ bunch fresh broccoli,
*   washed and cut into*
*   1-inch florets, then cooked*
*   al dente*
freshly ground black pepper
1 tablespoon butter
½ cup freshly grated cheese,
*   half romano and half*
*   parmesan*

3. Cook the pasta *al dente,* drain well, and return it to the pan in which it cooked. Add the butter and toss lightly. Add the olive oil and broccoli mixture and toss again. Add the cheeses and toss once more. Serve at once.

VARIATION
Add ½ teaspoon red pepper flakes to the skillet as you remove it from the heat.

Tomato Sauce with Butter

1. If using fresh tomatoes, wash them well, cut each in half, and cook over low heat in a covered pan for 15 minutes. Put them through a food mill to have a fine purée. If using canned tomatoes, measure 2 cups into a food mill along with about ½ cup of juice in the can and process for a fine purée.

2. In a medium saucepan, place the butter, onion and carrot pieces, sugar, and salt. Add the tomato purée. Over low heat simmer these ingredients for 40 minutes, uncovered. Stir frequently and be sure the simmer does not turn to a boil.

SERVES 4
for ½ pound any pasta

INGREDIENTS
2 pounds ripe plum tomatoes or 2 cups canned Italian plum tomatoes
¼ pound butter, cut into 8 pieces
1 medium onion, peeled and quartered
1 medium carrot, peeled and quartered
¼ teaspoon sugar
1½ teaspoons salt

3. Remove onion and carrot pieces, adjust sauce for salt seasoning, and serve over freshly cooked pasta.

NOTE
This sauce may be made ahead and reheated and freezes very well. The reserved onion and carrot pieces may be served on the side of the pasta dish or left to be eaten cold later, as an appetizer. There won't be much to go around, but they are flavorful and delicious and should not be discarded.

Tomato Sauce with Vegetables

1. Prepare a tomato purée as directed in the previous recipe. In a medium saucepan combine the tomatoes with the onion, carrot, celery, and parsley pieces. Add the sugar and salt and simmer for 30 minutes over low heat. Do not cover pan. Stir frequently.

2. When the vegetables are cooked, transfer to a food mill or food processor and purée the mixture. Return this mixture to the pan in which it cooked.

SERVES 4
for ½ pound any pasta

INGREDIENTS
*2 pounds ripe plum tomatoes
  or 2 cups canned Italian
  plum tomatoes
⅔ cup chopped onion
  (½-inch cubes)
⅔ cup chopped carrot
  (½-inch cubes)
⅔ cup chopped celery,
  including pale green leaves
  (½-inch pieces)
2 tablespoons finely chopped
  flat parsley
½ teaspoon sugar
1½ teaspoons salt
½ cup olive oil*

3. Add the olive oil to the tomato/vegetable mixture and over low heat simmer for 15 minutes. Do not cover pan. Stir several times with a wooden spoon or rubber spatula to clean the sides of the pan. Serve over freshly cooked pasta.

Tomato Sauce with Sautéed Vegetables

1. Prepare a tomato purée as directed on page 7. Set aside. In a large skillet, heat the olive oil and butter until bubbly. Add the onion, celery, and carrot and sauté for 10 minutes until the onion becomes opaque and the other vegetables begin to turn color. Use low heat and be careful not to brown or scorch the vegetables.

SERVES 4
for ½ pound any thin pasta

INGREDIENTS

2 pounds ripe plum tomatoes or 2 cups canned Italian plum tomatoes
⅓ cup olive oil
3 tablespoons butter
½ cup finely chopped onion
⅓ cup finely chopped celery, including pale green leaves
⅓ cup finely chopped carrot
½ teaspoon sugar
1 teaspoon salt

2. Add tomato purée to the skillet along with the sugar and salt. Cook uncovered at a bare simmer for 40 minutes. Stir frequently and be sure the sauce does not begin to boil. Serve over freshly cooked pasta.

Filetto Sauce

1. In a large saucepan, heat the oil, add the garlic, and sauté just until it begins to color (only a minute or two). Add the onions and sauté until they become opaque. Add the salt, oregano, basil, and red pepper flakes. Stir well.

2. Add the tomatoes and sugar, bring to a boil, lower heat, and simmer uncovered for 30 minutes. Stir every 5 minutes or so. Taste for seasoning and add pepper as you wish.

NOTE

This is a light tomato sauce and it should not be overcooked. It's a very popular sauce in Italy. If you recall seeing the restaurant staff eating pasta in the back room of the *trattoria,* the chances are that the sauce was this one. It's flavorful because of the combination of

SERVES 5 TO 6
for 1 pound shells or other substantial pasta

INGREDIENTS

2 tablespoons olive oil
2 cloves garlic, chopped fine
2 large onions, chopped fine
¾ teaspoon salt
1 teaspoon fresh oregano or
  ⅓ teaspoon dried
2 tablespoons fresh basil or 2
  teaspoons dried
¼ teaspoon red pepper flakes
1½ pounds ripe plum
  tomatoes, peeled, seeded,
  and chopped (or a
  2-pound can of Italian
  plum tomatoes, put
  through a food mill)
½ teaspoon sugar
freshly ground black pepper

garlic and onion, oregano and basil. Tomato paste or tomato purée should not be substituted. It is very easy to double or even triple this recipe for freezing.

VARIATION

To make a stronger garlic-tomato sauce which is very good with large macaroni (for example, ziti) or wide noodles, heat 4 tablespoons of oil and sauté 8 cloves of garlic. Add 8 fresh basil leaves (or ½ teaspoon dried), the filetto sauce, and ½ cup red and ¼ cup marsala wines and cook over low heat at a simmer for 10 minutes. Cook the pasta, drain, and return it to the pan in which it cooked. Add 3 tablespoons of butter and toss well. Add ½ of the sauce and ½ cup of parmesan cheese, and toss well. Pass remaining sauce and cheese at table.

Quick Ragù Bolognese

1. In a large skillet, heat the butter and oil and sauté the mushroom slices for 2 minutes. Remove with a slotted spoon and transfer to a medium saucepan.

2. Add the garlic and sauté for 1 minute. Add the chicken livers and sauté until they are light brown on the outside, pink on the inside (slice or cut through a piece to see). Transfer livers and garlic to the saucepan with the mushrooms.

3. In the skillet add the ground meat, season to taste with salt and pepper, and cook 6 minutes over medium heat, breaking up the meat as it cooks. The meat should be pink. Transfer to the saucepan. Add the filetto sauce to the saucepan and simmer for 5 minutes.

SERVES 4 TO 6
for 1 pound any pasta except very thin

INGREDIENTS
1 tablespoon butter
2 tablespoons olive oil
6 fresh mushrooms, sliced thin
2 cloves garlic, peeled and chopped fine
8 chicken livers, washed and dried, trimmed, and coarsely chopped
1 pound ground top sirloin
salt and pepper
3 cups Filetto Sauce (page 37)
½ cup heavy cream
1 cup parmesan cheese

4. Stir in the cream and when the sauce is hot, toss half of it with hot cooked pasta. Add ½ cup of cheese; toss again. Serve the remaining sauce spooned on top of the individual servings and divide the rest of the cheese among the pasta servings.

NOTE
Filetto sauce is basic to Italian cooking and has the advantage of being extended for use as another sauce. Here, its versatility is adapted to a quick *ragù bolognese*.

For most dishes, 2 cups of sauce are adequate for 1 pound of pasta. The remainder may be refrigerated, tightly covered, for 3 to 4 days or successfully frozen for future use.

Ragù Bolognese

Ragù bolognese is a meat sauce for seasoning homemade pasta. Although it requires long cooking, it is well worth it. Some consider the marriage of pasta with ragù bolognese to be made in heaven and we agree; use the sauce with any size pasta, but follow the directions carefully for there are some fundamental techniques; after all, it's not that easy to get to heaven.

1. Melt the butter in a 10- to 12-inch saucepan or 2-quart enameled or stainless-steel casserole. Add the vegetables (the *soffritto,* as the Italians call it) and cook, stirring frequently, for about 10 minutes or until the vegetables are lightly brown.

2. Add the ground meat, mashing it into the *soffritto* with a large spoon, and continuing to mix until all the lumps have disappeared and the meat has broken up into bits. Raise the heat and cook for about 3 minutes until the meat begins to lose color.

MAKES 3½ TO 4 CUPS

INGREDIENTS

6 tablespoons butter
1 cup coarsely chopped onion
½ cup coarsely chopped celery
¼ cup coarsely chopped carrot
½ pound lean beef chuck and ¾ pound lean pork, ground together twice through the finest blade of a meat grinder
½ cup dry white wine
1 cup milk
1 pound ripe tomatoes, peeled, seeded, and finely chopped (1½ cups), or 1½ cups drained and finely chopped canned Italian plum tomatoes
1 tablespoon finely chopped fresh parsley
salt
freshly ground black pepper
freshly grated nutmeg

3. Add the wine, bring it to a boil, and, stirring constantly, cook until it has almost completely evaporated. Stir in the milk and cook until the milk has almost evaporated.

4. Add the chopped tomatoes, bring sauce to a boil again, then reduce the heat to its lowest point. Half-cover the pan or casserole and simmer the sauce for 3 hours, stirring every now and then. By this time, most of the liquid will have cooked away and the sauce should be thick and intensely flavored. Add the parsley.

5. Taste for seasoning and add as much salt, pepper, and nutmeg as desired. The sauce may now be used exactly as it is.

Quick Tomato Sauce with Marsala

1. Put the tomatoes through a food mill. Do not use a blender. A food mill will purée the pulp and get rid of the seeds; a blender chops the seeds along with the tomatoes.

2. In a large skillet or medium saucepan, melt the butter and cook the onions until soft. Add the garlic, tomato purée, and crumbled bacon. Then add salt and pepper to taste. Boil this sauce hard for 3 minutes.

SERVES 4
for ½ pound of any pasta

INGREDIENTS
*2 cups fresh peeled plum
  tomatoes or canned Italian
  plum tomatoes*
2 tablespoons butter
2 small onions, chopped fine
1 clove garlic, chopped fine
*4 slices bacon, cooked and
  crumbled*
salt
freshly ground black pepper
½ cup marsala wine
½ teaspoon dried oregano

3. Add the marsala and oregano, and cook for another 5 minutes. Serve over hot cooked pasta.

On the following pages: Peas with Pasta Shells (recipe on page 94); Herb-Speckled Pasta (recipe on page 64).

Tomato Sauce with Beef

1. In a heavy saucepan, heat the oil and sauté the carrot for 2 minutes. Add the onion and garlic and cook over high heat for 3 minutes. Add the meat, and cook over high heat for about 5 minutes until the red color disappears.

SERVES 8
for 1½ pounds string or heavier pasta

INGREDIENTS
1 tablespoon olive oil
1 small carrot, chopped fine
1 small onion, chopped fine
1 clove garlic, chopped fine
1 pound good-quality ground chuck
½ cup red wine
1 teaspoon sugar
6 cups ripe plum or canned Italian plum tomatoes (including pulp and liquid), put through food mill to remove seeds (see page 7.)
1 tablespoon finely chopped fresh basil or ½ teaspoon dried
1 tablespoon tomato paste
1½ teaspoons salt
freshly ground black pepper

2. Add the wine, sugar, puréed tomatoes, basil, tomato paste, salt, and pepper to taste. Lower the heat to moderate, bring to boil, and simmer half-covered for 1½ hours. Stir frequently, every 10 minutes or so, then serve over hot cooked pasta.

Fresh Tomato Sauce (Uncooked)

1. Place tomatoes in a bowl. Add all other ingredients and mix well.

2. Cook, drain, and sauce the pasta with half the mixture. Toss and add remaining sauce. Serve immediately.

SERVES 4
for 1 pound of any pasta

INGREDIENTS
3 large ripe tomatoes, peeled, seeded, and cut into ½-inch pieces
1 clove garlic, peeled and chopped fine
1 small onion, peeled and chopped fine
8 large basil leaves, washed, dried, and chopped fine (or 1 teaspoon dried basil)
1 tablespoon finely chopped fresh oregano or ½ teaspoon dried
1 teaspoon finely chopped fresh rosemary or ½ teaspoon dried (chopped fine or rubbed between palm of hands)
1½ teaspoons salt
freshly ground black pepper
½ cup olive oil
juice from 1 lemon, strained

NOTE
This sauce can be prepared ahead of time and may be held at room temperature for as long as half a day. If made the day before, refrigerate the sauce but bring it to room temperature before adding to hot pasta. Although this sauce is best served as described above, we have taken this pasta dish in a covered casserole to picnic grounds and to the beach and it was delicious.

Marinara Sauce

1. Barely heat the olive oil and butter in a heavy 10-inch skillet. Add the onion and, stirring occasionally, cook over low heat for 10 minutes until soft and opaque but not brown. Stir in the carrot, cook for 4 minutes longer; add the basil, parsley, and bay leaf. Simmer a moment or two, stirring constantly.

2. Add the tomatoes with their liquid. Raise the heat and bring the mixture to a boil, meanwhile mashing and breaking up the tomatoes with the back of a large spoon. Stir in the tomato paste and a liberal grinding of pepper. Cook the sauce over moderate heat (it should cook fairly briskly, not simmer) for 30 to 45 minutes, or until most of the liquid in the pan has evaporated and the sauce has become a coarse purée thick enough to hold its shape lightly in a spoon. Watch carefully for any signs of burning and lower the heat if necessary.

SERVES 4 TO 6
for 1 pound of any pasta

INGREDIENTS
2 tablespoons olive oil
2 tablespoons butter
1 cup finely chopped onion
½ cup finely chopped carrot
2 teaspoons crumbled dried basil
2 tablespoons finely chopped flat parsley
1 medium bay leaf
1 can (2 pounds 3 ounces) Italian plum tomatoes
1 tablespoon tomato paste
freshly ground black pepper
3 flat anchovy filets, drained, rinsed in cold water and finely chopped, about 1 teaspoon
¼ teaspoon hot red pepper flakes
salt

3. Purée the sauce in a food mill (not a blender, which would liquify it too much). Discard any vegetables remaining in the mill or sieve and return the sauce to the pan. Bring it to a simmer over low heat; stir in the anchovies and the pepper flakes. There should be about 2 cups of smooth, thick sauce in the pan; if there is more, and it seems thin or watery, boil rapidly uncovered until it thickens and has boiled down to about 2 cups. Stir frequently and watch for burning. Adjust salt seasoning.

VARIATION
Add ½ pound Italian sausages (hot or sweet) to 2 cups of marinara sauce. Boil sausages in any vessel after you have pierced them in several places. Cook over moderate heat for 6 minutes, remove, drain, and dry them. Cut on bias into thin slices and heat with marinara sauce.

Pesto Sauce

1. In the mixing bowl of a food processor or blender, put the garlic, salt, basil, pinenuts and olive oil, and process until smooth, scraping down sides one or two times.

2. Add the cheeses and butter and process very briefly, just to incorporate the cheeses and butter.

3. Add 2 tablespoons of the boiling water in which the pasta cooked. If sauce is still too thick, add a little more boiling water. Process for 1 or 2 seconds. The sauce is now ready for the cooked pasta.

NOTE

If you want to use a mortar and pestle, combine the garlic, salt, basil, and pinenuts and grind them first. Then add the cheeses and mix with a fork or wooden spoon. Add the oil a little at a time and finally incorporate the soft

SERVES 4 TO 6
for 1 pound thin pasta

INGREDIENTS

2 cloves garlic, peeled
1 teaspoon salt
2 cups tightly packed fresh basil leaves
2 tablespoons finely chopped pinenuts
½ cup olive oil
½ cup freshly grated parmesan cheese
2 tablespoons freshly grated romano cheese
4 tablespoons butter, softened

butter. Be sure to thin with at least 2 tablespoons of boiling pasta water.

When draining the pasta, just before mixing with the pesto sauce, allow the pasta to be moist with water; in other words, don't shake out colander to rid the pasta of all the liquid. In combining the pasta with pesto, put pesto first in a warm bowl, add the pasta and toss it well to coat the strands. Or if you want to do this *Genoese* style, put the pasta on individual serving plates. Sprinkle some cheese and put 1 or more tablespoons of pesto in the center (make a well) of each pasta serving.

Since pesto freezes well, you can make pesto with fresh basil leaves when they are available and therefore substitutions are really not necessary. We do not know how anyone can make pesto with dried basil, but we have tasted an acceptable "pesto" when fresh parsley has been used instead of fresh basil.

Anchovy Sauce

1. In a skillet, heat the oil and add the crushed garlic cloves. Sauté until they are a very light tan, then remove and discard them. Do not let the cloves cook longer than light beige or tan. Add the anchovy filet pieces and, with a fork or wooden spoon, stir until they dissolve in the oil.

2. Add the red pepper flakes and parsley pieces. Stir well and remove skillet from the heat. Pour the sauce over freshly cooked and drained pasta, and toss well to coat the strands.

SERVES 4
for 1 pound of vermicelli or thin spaghetti

INGREDIENTS
½ cup + 1 tablespoon olive oil
2 cloves garlic, mashed and peeled
2 anchovy filets, chopped in ¼-inch pieces
¼ teaspoon red pepper flakes
2 tablespoons finely chopped flat parsley

NOTE
The easiest way to peel garlic is to put the cloves on a flat surface, make a fist, and come down heel-side first on the clove. With the right amount of force, you'll "break open" the clove, which then is easy to peel. We grew up hearing this "thud" in the kitchen, and it's one of those never-fail little "trucs."

Balsamella Sauce

This sauce is essential to many baked and stuffed pastas such as lasagne. It is easy to make and takes only several minutes. If you use a wire whisk, you'll avoid lumps; the sauce must be smooth.

1. In a small saucepan, melt the butter over moderate heat without letting it brown. Remove the pan from the heat, add the flour, and stir together thoroughly.

2. Add the milk and the cream, and beat with a whisk to dissolve the flour partially. Then return the pan to moderate heat and, whisking constantly, bring the sauce to a boil. When it is quite thick and smooth, reduce the heat to its lowest point and simmer the sauce for 2 or 3 minutes to remove any taste of raw flour. Stir in the salt, pepper, and nutmeg.

MAKES ABOUT 1 CUP

INGREDIENTS
3 tablespoons butter
3 tablespoons flour
½ cup milk
½ cup heavy cream
½ teaspoon salt
pinch of white pepper
pinch of nutmeg

3. If the sauce is not to be used right away, stir it every now and then as it cools to prevent a skin from forming on its surface. Cover it with plastic wrap and refrigerate; it will solidify when cold. Reheat it to tepid, stirring constantly, before using. Thin it with a little more milk or cream if it seems too thick.

PASTA IN COLORS

*M*an and woman have an innate love of change and this is so seen in the Italian kitchen when it comes to pastas. For only so long a time could one be contented with just pasta without eggs and pasta with eggs, both of which are pale and lemon colored. In the fanciful book, *L'Osservatore Fiorentino* written by Laschi, he commented that "It would not seem that the senses should be subjected to fashion; and yet such is the case—whoever characterized man as a laughing animal ought rather to have called him a variable and inconstant one." For pasta has changed and these days, to satisfy the quest for Italian ingenuity, pasta is being kneaded and rolled into all colors of the rainbow. What is not surprising at all is that these colored pastas taste delicious in addition to looking so "fashionable." The piselli (pea) pasta described later is beautiful to the eye but, more importantly, it raises one's sense of taste to a new high and its lightness is ethereal. And from there we have yellow pastas, pounded and compounded with lemon zest or saffron, to orange-colored pastas ignited by carrots, tomatoes, or oranges. Green pastas are not limited to spinach. We've moved it on to broccoli and peas; but you could experiment with leeks, chard, or escarole. Then there are the speckled and whole-wheat pastas. Each pasta in color has its own special sauce, a sauce complimenting the pasta color, its taste, and its texture.

Is it any wonder? Italians love pasta, Italians love color. This marriage had to be.

Lemon Pasta

Although this pasta resembles regular egg pasta noodles, it has a unique taste and a lemony flavor that comes through.

1. Use a large bowl with a wide opening or work on a large flat countertop. Make a well in the flour; add the eggs, lemon zest, lemon juice, salt, and olive oil. Using your hands, work the dough together. Add 1 or 2 tablespoons of water and keep working the dough until it forms a ball. If you need more water, add some to the dough.

2. Turn the dough out onto a lightly floured board. Knead it, adding more flour if necessary. Knead for about 10 minutes.

MAKES 1 POUND

INGREDIENTS
2½–3 cups all-purpose flour
2 eggs, lightly beaten
2 tablespoons minced lemon
  zest
3 tablespoons strained lemon
  juice
½ teaspoon salt
1 tablespoon olive oil
3 or 4 tablespoons warm
  water

3. Cover the ball with a bowl or cloth and let the dough rest for 30 minutes.

4. Follow the directions for rolling out and shaping pasta on page 11.

Lemon Pasta with Fresh Clams

1. In a large saucepan, add the clams and ⅓ cup of wine or vermouth. Cover the pan and, on medium high, boil the clams until they open, about 5 or 8 minutes. Do not overcook. Discard any clams that have not opened.

2. Let clams cool and remove clams from their shells and set aside.

3. Strain the clam broth through a double piece of cheesecloth and reserve. You will have about ¾ cup to 1 cup of broth.

4. In a large skillet add the oil and butter and heat for a few seconds. Add the shallots and garlic and sauté briefly. Add the reserved wine, clam broth, oregano, red pepper flakes, and parsley. Simmer for 10 minutes.

5. Add the clams and cook for 2 minutes. Do not overcook the clams or they will toughen.

SERVES 4

INGREDIENTS

3 dozen small hard-shell clams (littlenecks or cherrystones), scrubbed and cleaned
⅔ cup dry white wine or ⅔ cup dry vermouth
¼ cup olive oil
2 tablespoons butter
2 teaspoons finely chopped shallots
2 cloves garlic, chopped fine
1 teaspoon fresh oregano or ½ teaspoon dried
½ teaspoon red pepper flakes
2 teaspoons finely chopped fresh parsley
½ pound Lemon Pasta
¼ cup freshly grated parmesan cheese
salt
1 tablespoon finely chopped lemon zest

6. Cook the pasta until *al dente*. Add the sauce and clams to the pasta and mix a little. Add the cheese and mix well. Taste and add salt to taste. Serve in individual bowls or a large platter. Add the lemon zest over all.

WINE
An albana secco, or other light, fresh white wine

Saffron Pasta

This special pasta is orange in color and may be made even deeper in tone by adding more saffron. It combines admirably with vegetable sauces.

1. In a large bowl, add the flour, salt, and saffron; mix well to distribute the color evenly. Make a well in the center of the flour, add the eggs and oil, and work the dough together.

2. Add the water and work the dough until it forms a ball. Transfer to a lightly floured board and knead for 5 minutes.

3. Cover the dough with a bowl and let it rest for 20 minutes. Use a manual pasta machine (see page 12), or roll it out by hand (page 11).

MAKES ¾ TO 1 POUND

INGREDIENTS
1½ cups all-purpose flour
½ teaspoon salt
large pinch of ground or
    pulverized saffron
2 eggs
2 tablespoons olive oil
1 tablespoon water

NOTE
Use this pasta with any of the butter sauces on pages 29–32, or with most of the recipes on pages 84–102.

Saffron Pasta with Green Peas, Mint, and Scallions

This is a great summertime dish if you can pick fresh peas, scallions, and mint from your garden.

1. Heat the butter in a large skillet and add the vermouth. Cook for several minutes until the vermouth thickens and deglazes the pan.

2. Add the chicken broth and bring to a boil. Add the peas and scallions, turn the heat to high for 2 minutes, then remove from heat and set aside.

3. Cook the saffron pasta bows until *al dente;* drain and return the pasta to the pan in which it cooked. Add the chicken broth

SERVES 3 TO 4

INGREDIENTS

2 tablespoons butter
¼ cup dry vermouth
1 cup chicken broth
1 cup fresh or frozen green peas (if fresh, parboil and drain; if frozen, boil to thaw and drain)
½ cup chopped fresh scallions, including tender green parts
½ pound Saffron Pasta, preferably bowties
2 tablespoons finely chopped fresh mint, or 1 teaspoon dried
salt and black pepper

and green pea sauce, along with the mint, salt, and pepper to taste. Toss well and serve.

WINE

A riesling from Friuli, or other full-bodied white wine

51

Orange Pasta, "Arancia"

Pale, beautiful orange-colored pasta, as light as any pasta can be. The orange flavor is refreshing.

1. Use a large bowl with a wide opening. Add the flour and make a well in the center. Add the eggs, olive oil, and orange zest. Add orange juice 1 tablespoon at a time, then add salt. Using your hands or 2 wooden spoons, work the dough together gathering all the flour from the sides of the bowl. Add more orange juice and keep working until it forms a ball.

2. Turn the dough out onto a lightly floured board and start kneading. If you need more flour, use it. Knead for about 10 minutes, then cover the dough with a bowl or cloth and let it rest for 30 minutes.

3. Follow instructions for using the manual pasta machine (page 12).

MAKES 1½ POUNDS

INGREDIENTS
3 cups all-purpose flour
3 eggs, at room temperature, beaten lightly
1 tablespoon olive oil
2 tablespoons minced orange zest
3 or 4 tablespoons strained orange juice
½ teaspoon salt

NOTE
This pasta combines well with vegetables—see the recipes for pasta with artichokes (pages 86–87); with cauliflower (page 89); and with ricotta sauce (page 81).

Orange Pasta with Spinach Slivers, Mushrooms, and Cream

1. Carefully wash the spinach leaves to remove all sand. Also remove stems. Spin dry or wipe the leaves dry and shred into thinnest possible slivers. (This is best done by hand with a good knife.) Set aside.

2. Wipe the mushrooms with kitchen toweling and cut off the stem ends. (Reserve stem ends for stock.) Slice the mushrooms thinly and, in a small bowl, mix the lemon and the mushrooms, tossing them well.

3. In a skillet, melt the butter and add the garlic and marsala. Cook for 3 minutes, then add the mushrooms. Cook for 5 minutes and then add the cream. Bring to a boil; add some salt and pepper liberally. Remove from the heat.

SERVES 4

INGREDIENTS
4 cups fresh spinach leaves
½ pound fresh mushrooms
juice of 1 lemon
4 tablespoons butter
1 clove garlic, chopped fine
2 tablespoons marsala wine
1 cup heavy cream
salt
freshly ground black pepper
¾ pound Orange Pasta
4 heaping tablespoons freshly grated parmesan cheese

4. Cook the pasta until *al dente* (remember it cooks fast). Drain thoroughly and return it to the pot in which it cooked. Add the sauce to the pasta and toss lightly. Add the fresh spinach pieces, toss lightly, again. Serve with the freshly grated parmesan cheese.

WINE
A chianti classico or another dry, medium red wine

Carrot Pasta

This pasta will not have a carrot-looking color. It will be paler, looking more like egg pasta with an orange tint.

1. In a medium bowl, add 2 cups of flour, make a well in the center and add the egg, olive oil, salt, carrots, and water. Mix well to make a dough.

2. Transfer the dough onto a floured board and knead for about 15 minutes, adding some of the reserved flour as needed. Work the dough into a ball, cover it with a bowl, and let it rest for 15 minutes.

3. Roll the dough into a cylinder about 6 or 7 inches long, and then slice it into ½-inch pieces. Flatten the pieces of pasta dough slightly with a rolling pin or the palm of your hand. See pages 11–19 for how to roll and cut the dough; see page 11 for how to roll pasta by hand.

MAKES 1 POUND

INGREDIENTS
2½ cups all-purpose flour
1 egg
1 tablespoon olive oil
1 teaspoon salt
2 carrots, chopped, cooked, and puréed (⅔ cup)
5 tablespoons warm water, or more if needed

NOTE
If the pasta is not being used within 2 days, put it in a plastic bag and freeze it; it freezes well. Carrot pasta is excellent with mushrooms, prosciutto, and cream as given on page 92 and also with green peas, basil, and scallions on page 95.

Carrot Pasta with Asparagus

1. In a medium pan, add 2 cups of water and let it come to a fast boil. Add the asparagus and cook it for 2 minutes only. Do not over-cook; the asparagus should be *al dente,* and have a bright green color. Drain and set aside.

2. Into a 4-quart saucepan, add the cream and cook it over low heat until it is half the original volume and it is thickened lightly (or thick enough to coat a spoon); this will take about 10 minutes. Cover the pan with wax paper and set aside.

3. Into a large pot place 6 quarts of water and let it come to a fast boil. Add the pasta and cook over high heat for 2 minutes; do not over cook. Drain the pasta well and return it to the pot in which it cooked.

SERVES 4 TO 6

INGREDIENTS
1 pound fresh asparagus, washed and trimmed, then cut on bias into 2-inch lengths
3 cups heavy cream
1 pound Carrot Pasta
salt
freshly ground black pepper
2 tablespoons finely chopped basil, or 1 teaspoon dried
½ cup freshly grated parmesan cheese

4. Add half the cream along with the salt and pepper. Mix well with 2 wooden forks, then add half the asparagus, saving the tips for the last step. Add the remaining cream, the basil, and the cheese and toss well.

5. Transfer the pasta to a large attractive platter. Add the asparagus tips on the top of the pasta. Serve at once and pass more cheese.

WINE
A chianti classico or other dry medium red wine

Tomato Pasta

This produces a pasta light orange in color—a soft shade that is pale and beautiful. It truly is one of the delights of the Italian kitchen.

1. Cook the tomatoes in a saucepan for 25 minutes or until all juices have evaporated and the pulp is thick. Put the cooked tomatoes in a food mill and purée. You should have about ⅔ cup. Allow to cool completely.

2. In a large bowl add the flour, salt, and tomato purée. Mix well with a wooden spoon or wisk, or by hand. Add the beaten eggs and mix until the dough comes together.

3. Transfer dough to a lightly floured board. Sprinkle with a little more flour, incorporating it as you knead the dough. Knead for at least 5 minutes. Cover the dough with a bowl and let rest for 20 minutes.

MAKES ¾ TO 1 POUND

INGREDIENTS
2 large fresh tomatoes or 3 medium, peeled, seeded, and chopped coarsely
2¼ cups all-purpose flour
salt
3 eggs, lightly beaten

4. Use a manual pasta machine for rolling and cutting (see page 12), or roll out by hand (page 11).

NOTE
This pasta can also be made successfully with 3 tablespoons of tomato paste instead of fresh tomatoes.

On the following pages: Baked Fettuccine (recipe on page 133); Zucchini and Farfalloni (recipe on page 99); Minestrone (recipe on page 179); Porcini and Tomatoes with Spinach Pasta (recipe on page 93).

Tomato Pasta with Tomato Sauce

The tomato sauce is one of the lightest, best tasting, and most refreshing sauces. It is beautifully combined with the tomato pasta, and, in addition to its taste, this combination creates a sensational visual dish—tomato on tomato, if you will.

1. Prepare the tomato sauce and keep it hot.

2. Cook the pasta until *al dente* and return it to the pan in which it cooked. Add half the sauce and toss with the pasta until the strands are coated.

SERVES 4

INGREDIENTS
1 recipe Tomato Sauce with Butter (page 34)
½ to ¾ pound Tomato Pasta
½ cup freshly grated parmesan cheese

3. Serve the pasta in individual bowls or a large platter and pour a little more of the remaining sauce on top. Pass the remaining sauce at the table and sprinkle with parmesan cheese.

WINE
A chianti classico, or other medium red wine

Beet Pasta

This pink pasta will not be the color of beets; it will be paler. You can make it a lighter pink or darker red by adding less or more beet purée.

1. In a medium bowl, add 3 cups of flour and make a well in the center. Add the eggs, olive oil, salt, and beet purée. Mix well to make a dough.

2. Transfer the dough onto a floured board and knead for about 15 minutes, adding some of the reserved flour as needed. Work the dough into a ball, cover it with a bowl, and let it rest for 15 minutes.

3. Roll the dough into a cylinder about 6 or 7 inches long, and then slice it into ½-inch pieces. Flatten the pieces of pasta dough slightly with a rolling pin or the palm of your hand. See page 12

MAKES 1 POUND

INGREDIENTS

3 to 3½ cups all-purpose flour
4 eggs
2 tablespoons olive oil
1 teaspoon salt
2 small beets, cooked and puréed

for instructions on rolling and cutting the dough; see page 11 for directions on how to roll pasta by hand.

NOTE

This pasta freezes well; put it in a plastic bag and store for up to 1 month.

Pink Pasta with Dill Sauce

1. In a mixing bowl or a food processor, whisk the egg yolk or process it until it is lemon colored and thick. Add the olive oil in a thin stream, then add the vegetable oil also in a thin stream, whisking or processing constantly until mixture thickens to consistency of mayonnaise.

2. Add the tarragon, garlic, salt, and pepper. Add the lemon juice and heavy cream and stir well or process for 2 seconds.

3. Add the sour cream and whisk until well combined. If using a food processor, remove the top, add the sour cream, put back the top, and whisk for 2 seconds until the sauce is well blended.

4. Cook the pasta until *al dente* and return it to the pan in which it cooked. Add the onion, beet, dill, and sauce and toss so that each strand of pasta is well coated.

SERVES 4 TO 6

INGREDIENTS
1 egg yolk
¼ cup olive oil
½ cup vegetable oil
2 teaspoons finely chopped fresh tarragon, or 1 teaspoon dried
1 clove garlic, chopped fine
salt
freshly ground black pepper
juice of ½ lemon
3 tablespoons heavy cream
½ cup sour cream
1 pound Beet Pasta
1 medium red onion, cut in very thin slices and then quartered
1 cooked beet, cut in ¼-inch dice
3 large sprigs fresh dill, chopped fine

5. Serve in individual bowls or a large platter and garnish with some more dill, cut into tiny featherlike pieces.

WINE
A dry white wine such as orvieto classico

Piselli Pasta

This is a truly exciting and different pasta that's also easy to make.

1. In a small pan, bring ½ cup of water to a fast boil. Add the peas and, with a wooden fork, break them apart. Let the peas come to another fast boil and cook for 5 minutes. Drain well. Put the peas in a food mill and process until all the peas are puréed; you should have about ⅔ cup. Add butter and mix well.

2. In a large bowl, add the flour, eggs, olive oil, and salt. With your hands, a whisk, or 2 wooden spoons, start mixing and gathering all the flour from the sides of the bowl. When the dough has all come together, transfer it to a lightly floured board and knead for at least 5 minutes. Cover and let rest for 15 or 20 minutes.

3. Cut the dough in 4 pieces. Flatten 1 piece with the palms of your hands. (Be sure to cover the dough that is not being used.)

MAKES ABOUT 1½ POUNDS

INGREDIENTS
1 package (10 ounces) frozen peas
1 tablespoon butter, softened
3 cups all-purpose flour
3 eggs, lightly beaten
1 tablespoon olive oil
½ teaspoon salt

With a rolling pin, roll out the dough (using a little more flour if needed) into a rectangle about 16 by 14 inches, and about ¹⁄₁₆th inch thick. (When doing pea pasta, do not use a lot of flour. It is a lot easier to work with than regular pasta dough.) Roll it into a tight roll to resemble a jellyroll. Transfer roll to a lightly floured surface. Roll out remaining portions. Let dough dry for 10 minutes.

4. Transfer the rolled pasta onto a lightly floured work surface. Slice with a sharp knife. If you're making *tagliarini,* cut about ⅛ inch thick; cut it 2 or 3 inches wide for lasagne, or cut into whatever shape you wish.

NOTE
Piselli pasta freezes well and can be frozen up to 1 month. It can also be stored at room temperature for 2 to 3 days. Piselli pasta is most versatile and can be sauced with butter and olive oil sauces on pages 29–33.

Piselli Pasta with Three Vegetables

1. Add 1 cup water to a medium pan. Lay the carrot, zucchini, and asparagus neatly in a vegetable steamer and put it into the pan. Cover the pan, turn the heat to medium high, and steam the vegetables for 2 minutes. Remove the steamer and set aside for a few minutes.

2. Heat 1 tablespoon of butter in a small saucepan, add the garlic and shallots, and sauté briefly, about 1 minute. Add the prosciutto and sauté another 1 minute. Add the chicken stock. Heat and stir until hot, then set aside for a few minutes.

3. Cook the pasta only 2 or 3 minutes; watch it carefully. Drain pasta well, and return it to the pot in which it cooked. Working rather quickly, add the remaining butter and, with 2 wooden forks, lift and mix, lift and mix to coat the strands.

SERVES 4

INGREDIENTS

1 carrot, sliced thin
1 small zucchini, trimmed and sliced thin
10 asparagus, cut in 2-inch lengths
4 tablespoons butter
1 clove garlic, chopped fine
2 shallots, chopped fine
4 slices Italian prosciutto, cut into strips, ½ by 2 inches
¼ cup chicken stock
¼ cup heavy cream, heated
½ pound Piselli Pasta
½ cup freshly grated parmesan cheese
salt
freshly ground black pepper
1 heaping tablespoon finely chopped fresh basil, or 1 teaspoon dried

4. Add the cream and the mixture from the saucepan. Add half the vegetables with half the cheese and mix thoroughly. Transfer the pasta to a platter, add salt and pepper to taste, and add the remaining vegetables. Sprinkle the remaining cheese on top, then sprinkle with the fresh basil. Serve immediately.

WINE
A valpolicella or other dry red wine

Broccoli Pasta

1. In a small saucepan, add ½ cup of salted water and let it come to a fast boil. Add the broccoli and let it come to a second boil. Separate the broccoli with a fork to make it cook faster. When separated, cover and let cook over low heat for 4 to 6 minutes. Drain in a hand strainer and, when cool enough to handle, use your hands to press down and remove all the liquid.

2. In a large bowl with a wide top, add the flour and salt. Make a well in the center of the flour and add the eggs, broccoli, and oil. Using your hands or a whisk or a wooden fork, work the dough together. Keep working the dough until it forms a ball.

3. Turn the dough out onto a lightly floured board. Knead the dough, adding more flour if needed, until smooth. The kneading will take about 10 minutes.

MAKES 1½ POUNDS

INGREDIENTS

1 package (10 ounces) frozen chopped broccoli
3 cups all-purpose flour
½ teaspoon salt
2 large eggs, at room temperature
1 tablespoon olive oil

Cover with a bowl or cloth and let the dough rest for 30 minutes.

4. Using a little flour, roll the dough into a cylinder about 10 or 12 inches long. (It will look like a loaf of uncooked Italian bread.) Cut the dough into 12 pieces (about ¾ inches thick), flatten each piece with the palm of your hand, using more flour if needed. See page 12 for how to roll and cut the dough; see page 11 for how to roll pasta by hand.

NOTE
Broccoli pasta freezes well. Put it into a large plastic bag or a box big enough to hold the pasta. Cover with wax paper, seal the box, and freeze. This pasta excels when used in the primavera preparation on pages 100–101.

Broccoli Pasta with Garlic and Oil

1. In a medium pan over medium high, heat the oil for 3 minutes. Add the carrot and garlic and sauté briefly. Do not brown the garlic or it will have a bitter taste.

2. Add the wine and cook 4 minutes more. Add the salt and red pepper flakes. Turn off the heat and set aside.

3. Cook the pasta until *al dente*. Drain, but leave a few tablespoons of the water in the pan. Return the pasta to the pan in which it cooked.

4. Add butter, and mix until the butter is melted. Working fast, add the garlic and oil to the pasta, lifting and mixing. Add the cheese and mix again until well combined.

SERVES 4

INGREDIENTS

¹⁄₂ cup olive oil
1 small carrot, chopped fine
3 large cloves garlic, chopped fine
¹⁄₄ cup dry white wine or vermouth
salt
¹⁄₄–¹⁄₂ teaspoon red pepper flakes
¹⁄₂ pound Broccoli Pasta
2 tablespoons butter
¹⁄₄ cup freshly grated parmesan cheese

5. Serve in individual plates or in a large bowl or platter. Pass more cheese.

WINE
A young chianti classico

Herb-Speckled Pasta

This pasta is best made with fresh herbs cut as finely as possible. If you must use dried herbs, crush or blend them as finely as you can.

1. In a large bowl, place the flour and make a well in the center. Add the eggs, salt, olive oil, and water or milk. Then add the herbs and using your hands, work the dough together. Keep working until the dough forms a ball.

2. Turn the dough onto a lightly floured board and knead, adding more flour if needed, until smooth. The kneading will take about 10 minutes. Cover with a bowl or cloth and let the dough rest for 30 minutes.

3. Use a manual pasta machine, as described on page 12, and cut the pasta into fettuccine or any other string pasta you wish.

MAKES ¾ TO 1 POUND

INGREDIENTS

2¼ cups all-purpose flour
3 eggs
¾ teaspoon salt
1 tablespoon olive oil
1 tablespoon lukewarm water or milk
2 tablespoons finely chopped fresh parsley
1 tablespoon finely chopped fresh marjoram, or 1 teaspoon dried
2 tablespoons finely chopped fresh basil, or 1 teaspoon dried
1 tablespoon finely chopped fresh thyme, or 1 teaspoon dried

NOTE

The butter sauces on pages 29–32 are excellent with this pasta, as are the olive oil sauces on pages 32–33.

Herbed Pasta with Butter, Cheese, and Cream

1. In a heavy casserole, one that can be put over direct heat (it is best to use an enameled cast-iron casserole here), combine all the butter and half the cream. Over low heat, simmer until the butter and cream have melted. This should take less than 1 minute. Turn off the heat.

2. Cook the pasta for just a minute or so. Drain well, then transfer from the colander to the casserole with the butter and cream.

3. Turn the heat on under the casserole and, with 2 wooden spoons or forks, lift the pasta and toss well, coating completely with the sauce. Add the remaining cream, the parmesan cheese, salt and pepper to taste, and just a pinch of nutmeg. Toss briefly for another minute, making sure the pasta is well coated. Correct the seasoning and serve immediately with more grated cheese on the side.

SERVES 4

INGREDIENTS
8 tablespoons butter
1 cup heavy cream
1 pound Herb-speckled Pasta
*1 cup freshly grated parmesan
    cheese*
salt
freshly ground pepper
*pinch of freshly ground
    nutmeg*

WINE
A white sauvignon

Fresh Black Pepper Pasta

Of course this pasta has a peppery look and taste. It is better if the pepper is freshly ground. The spicy flavor does not interfere with its lightness.

1. Put the flour on a flat surface and shape it into a mound. Make a well in the center and add the eggs, salt, olive oil, 2 tablespoons water, and the ground pepper. (Be sure when you grind the pepper, it isn't too large or it will tear the pasta.) Mix with a wooden spoon by combining the eggs and the flour with a circular motion, taking some flour from the inside of the well. Add the remaining water and mix until it comes together.

2. Transfer the dough onto a floured board and knead it for 10 minutes. Work the dough into a ball, cover it with a bowl, and let it rest for 15 minutes.

MAKES ¾ POUND

INGREDIENTS
2 cups all-purpose flour
2 eggs, at room temperature
½ teaspoon salt
1 tablespoon olive oil
4 tablespoons water
*1 heaping tablespoon finely
  ground fresh pepper*

3. Roll the dough (using more flour if needed) into a cylinder about 6 inches long and slice into 1-inch pieces. Flatten each piece of dough with a rolling pin or the palm of your hand. Roll dough out on a pasta machine (see page 12).

NOTE
This pasta may be frozen for up to 1 month. All the butter sauces are extremely good with this pasta.

Black Pepper Pasta with Olive Oil and Broccoli Sauce

1. In a large skillet add the olive oil and the anchovies. Cook together until the anchovies combine with the oil; use a wooden spoon to dissolve the anchovies.

2. Add the broccoli florets and the pepper and sauté over moderate heat for 5 minutes. Check and adjust salt seasoning if necessary.

3. Cook pasta until *al dente,* drain well, and return it to the pot in which it cooked. Add the butter and toss lightly. Add the olive oil and broccoli mixture and toss

SERVES 4 TO 6

INGREDIENTS

½ cup olive oil
6 flat anchovy filets, chopped
  coarse
½ bunch fresh broccoli, cut
  into 1-inch florets and
  cooked al dente
freshly ground black pepper
salt (optional)
1 pound Black Pepper Pasta
1 tablespoon butter
½ cut freshly grated cheese,
  half romano and half
  parmesan

again. Add the cheeses and toss once more. Serve in individual portions or put all the pasta in a large bowl or platter.

WINE
A young chianti classico

Whole-Wheat Pasta

Whole-wheat pasta has a color and texture all its own. It is truly tasty when used in the pasta salads with olive oil, lemon juice, herbs, and uncooked tomatoes. Do not use it with a creamy salad dressing.

1. On a flat surface or in a wide bowl with a wide opening, combine the whole-wheat and all-purpose flours. Make a well in the center and add the eggs, salt, olive oil, and water. Using your hands, 2 wooden spoons, or a wire whisk, work the dough together, gathering the flour from the sides of the well. Keep working the dough until it forms a ball.

2. Turn the dough out onto a lightly floured board, adding more *all-purpose* flour if needed to keep dough from getting sticky. Work the dough until smooth and satiny; this will take about 10 minutes.

MAKES 1½ POUNDS

INGREDIENTS

1 cup whole-wheat flour
2 cups all-purpose flour
4 eggs, lightly beaten
½ teaspoon salt
1 tablespoon olive oil
3 tablespoons warm water

3. Use a pasta machine (see page 12) and feed it through *each* dial setting until very thin. Then feed the pasta through the cutting rollers of the size you wish—fettuccine or tagliatelle.

NOTE
When working with flour, it is hard to judge the exact amount of liquid to use. The amount of liquid that any flour can absorb varies with the moisture already in the flour. Therefore add the water a spoonfull at a time; if you need more, add it. This pasta can be stored in the freezer for up to 1 month.

Whole-Wheat Pasta with Sausage and Fennel

1. In a medium skillet on low heat, cook the sausage, breaking it up with a wooden fork into small pieces. Sauté until lightly browned, about 5 minutes. If you're using homemade sausage, you may have to add a small amount of olive oil; if it's store-bought, you'll have to remove some of the rendered fat. When the sausage is brown, add the fennel seeds and mix. Keep warm.

2. Beat the eggs in a medium bowl with a wire whisk until slightly thick.

3. Cook the pasta until *al dente; do not overcook.* Drain well and return the pasta to the pot in which it cooked. Add the butter and toss well. Add the beaten eggs and very quickly keep tossing. Add the sausage with fennel, the cheese, and salt to taste. Add fresh parsley on top of pasta and serve at once. Pass additional cheese.

SERVES 4

INGREDIENTS

4 ounces luganega sausage, casing removed
½ teaspoon crushed Italian fennel seeds
3 eggs
½ pound Whole-wheat Pasta (fettuccine)
½ cup freshly grated romano cheese
3 tablespoons butter
salt
1 heaping tablespoon chopped fresh parsley

WINE
A wine from the Valtellina, such as grumello or valgella—a dry, medium-bodied red wine

PASTA WITH CHEESE

*I*t is almost impossible to think of Italian cuisine without cheese. Cheese is used in soups, main courses, and desserts, but perhaps it is best known when paired with pasta. In fact, it is rare to find a pasta dish without cheese (usually only the fish sauces avoid cheese). *Fettuccine al Alfredo* is only one example of a cheese-pasta dish, but a quick glance through these pages will show quickly how often cheese is served with pasta. Parmesan is surely the best known, the most popular, and probably the best tasting. It is fun, however, to experiment with other cheeses; we list some popular Italian cheeses available now in the U.S.

ASIAGO: Comes from Vincenza, but also is made in Padua, Verona, and Trentome. A cow's milk cheese with a fat content of 30 percent, Asiago has the form of a small flat wheel and has a somewhat sharp flavor. It can be eaten at the end of a meal and is very good grated on certain pastas. It is made in the U.S. in 3 forms: fresh (soft), medium, and old. It is less expensive than parmesan and can be substituted in most pasta dishes except those which demand the delicate parmesan touch.

BEL PAESE: From Lombardy, this is made from pasteurized cow's milk and has a fat content of approximately 50 percent. Its form is a rather thick disk usually about 8 inches in diameter and approximately 2 inches thick. Bel paese has a mild fruity flavor and is excellent with valpolicella wine.

Bel paese means "beautiful country," and the cheese is one of the best known and most popular of the Italian table cheeses. It is the trade name of one of a group of soft, mild, fast-ripened Italian cheeses. The first bel paese was made in Melzo, near Milan; on the lid of each box of bel paese there is a map of Italy with Melzo marked larger than Rome. Although intended as a table cheese, bel paese also serves for cooking. Its softness makes it an excellent melting cheese. A version of bel paese is now made in the U.S. in Wisconsin. It may be used in any recipe calling for mozzarella.

CACCIOCAVALLO: Its name means "cheese on horseback," and one theory is that the cheeses which are tied in pairs and hung over poles to cure look as though they were hung over a saddle. If the cheese is to be eaten straight, it is matured for 2 to 4 months, but if it is to be grated and used in cooking, it needs up to 12 months. The cheese has a smooth firm texture and a pleasant sharpish flavor; it keeps and travels well.

FIORE SARDO: Also known as pecorino sardo, this comes from Sardinia but also may be found in Latium and Campagna. It is made from sheep's milk and has a fat content of about 45 percent. Fiore sardo comes in small cylindrical wheels with convex rims about 8 inches in diameter and almost 6 inches high. It has a light, nutty flavor when young and much sharper taste as it is aged. It is excellent as a grated cheese or can be eaten at the end of a meal. It is similar to the other pecorinos such as romano.

FONTINA: This is one of the most delicious Italian cheeses. There are American imitations of this great Italian cheese, but they do not measure up to the original. The real fontina comes from the Piedmont's Val d'Aosta, a mountainous area just south of Switzerland. Fontina looks like Swiss gruyère; it has a rather light brown crust and comes in large wheels like swiss cheese, but it doesn't have the network of holes. Fontina is made from cow's milk and has a fat content of 45–50 percent; the flavor is delicate, somewhat fruity and it is excellent

Opposite: Spaghettini and Veal Birds in a Tomato Sauce (recipe on page 110). Following page: Spaghetti Frittata with Pancetta and Peas (recipe on page 115).

72

with the light, fruity wines of Piedmont. It is frequently melted so it is excellent with pasta dishes, especially those which require cheese for stuffing and baking. When fully cured, it is hard, and used for grating.

GORGONZOLA: The most popular of the Italian blue cheeses, gorgonzola is named after a village near Milan but is now mainly produced in and around Milan. Because gorgonzola keeps and travels well, it enjoys an international reputation; it is unique for its creaminess. White gorgonzola, slightly more bitter in flavor than the blue, is highly appreciated in Italy. It can also be found in the provinces of Cuomo, Cremona, Milano, and Pavia. Gorgonzola is made from cow's milk and has a fat content of 45 percent. It comes in a cylindrical form up to 12 inches in diameter and often as high as 8 inches. Very soft and tender, almost runny, it has a rather fully developed smell and a very savory taste. Gorgonzola can be used in sauces, with pasta, and at the end of the meal. It is excellent with a barolo wine.

MASCARPONE: A soft and delicate cow's milk cheese with creamy ricottalike consistency, this may be served as a dessert when mixed with sugar, coffee, cognac, or chartreuse. It is best in the autumn and winter. Good also in baked pasta dishes.

MOZZARELLA: A pure white, soft, smooth, and moist cheese made in pear, oval, square, or spherical shape. It has a mild and creamy, delicate and slightly sweet flavor; it is one of the most popular cheeses used in Italian cooking. Smoked mozzarella has been flavored by smoke, in many cases created artificially by chemicals instead of natural smoking over fire. It is delicious and works well in pasta salads.

Opposite: Pasta in Truffled Cream Sauce (recipe on page 98). Preceding page: Pasta Shells with Mascarpone Cheese and Walnuts (recipe on page 79).

PARMESAN: Grana cheese is the generic name of a group of Italian cheeses. The word *grana* means "grain" and refers to the grainy texture of the cheeses when they age. There are 2 types of grana cheeses, both commonly called parmesan outside of Italy: parmigiano-reggiano and grana paduano.

One of the finest cheeses in the world, parmesan has been made in Italy for more than 900 years. The full name is parmigiano-reggiano, and it comes from a small area of the country comprising Parma, from which it gets its name; Reggio-Emillia, where most of the cheese is produced; Modena; and certain sections of Bologna. It is made from mid-April to precisely November 11. Although parmesan can be eaten fresh, it is best known as a hard grating cheese which has the quality of bringing out the essence of every other ingredient with which it is matched. It is a cheese which has never been duplicated outside of Italy. In the U.S., parmesan cheese made in the Midwest is being sold in most supermarkets and a parmesan made in Argentina is finding its way into the delicatessen units of grocery stores; both are good, but we still prefer the Italian imported variety. Don't buy too much at a time, store it tightly wrapped in plastic in the refrigerator, and grate it each time you need it. This is extra work, but you'll appreciate the freshness of flavor and the moisture of newly grated cheese.

Parmesan cheese is made with cow's milk and has a fat content of 32 percent. It comes in large wheels with slightly convex sides, often up to 18 inches in diameter and 10 inches high. It is a hard, brittle, and crumbly cheese, very fruity to sharp flavor in taste. It is the cheese most commonly ground to go with pasta, but it may be cut and eaten at the end of a meal.

PECORINO ROMANO: *Pecorino* is a generic name for all Italian cheeses made with sheep's milk. *Pecorino romano* is a hard grating cheese used for pasta; *pecorino da tavola* is a sharp and pungent table cheese but milder than the grating pecorinos. Both have minimum fat content of 36 percent, and have a slightly smoky smell and a strong flavor with a sharp taste. They are excellent with full bodied wines from the south and Sicily. They are used as grated cheeses with pasta and may also be enjoyed at the end of meals. Often, romano is less expensive than parmesan; but remember, it has more of a bite.

PECORINO SICILIANO: Also known as *canestrato* ("draining basket"), this is one of the most popular of the Sicilian cheeses. A strongly flavored cheese, it is molded in baskets and hardened sufficiently to be grated. It is made from sheep's milk with a minimum fat content of 40 percent and comes in cylinders with flat sides, often 10 inches in diameter and as high as 7 inches. It is like the pecorino romano, again with a distinct smell characteristic of sheep's milk cheeses.

PROVOLONE: Provolone is associated with southern Italy, especially the Campania region. It is made from cow's milk and has a 44 percent fat content. With a smooth, glossy golden rind and a dense creamy-white inside, provolone can taste delicate but sharp also, depending on its age. It is eaten generally with appetizers or at the end of a meal, but can also be grated and used with pasta.

RICOTTA: A white, creamy cottage cheese made from the whey from other cheeses such as provolone, pecorino, and mozzarella. It is on the borderline of being a cheese, but is an important ingredient in much of Italy's cooking, used as a filling for ravioli and many lasagne and cannelloni dishes as well as for sweet dishes.

RICOTTA SALATA: This is a salty, dry, hard ricotta which is rather mild. It is grated and used as a seasoning. Because more liquid is drained away, it has the same consistency as feta cheese; it is not like ricotta.

ROMANO: See Pecorino romano.

SCAMORZE: Somewhat like provolone, this cheese from the Campania region of Italy may also be found in Abruzzi and Molise. It is made from cow's milk and has a fat content of 44 percent. Its interesting gourd shape with a narrow neck is tied with a cord with 4 little loops on top; it is mostly seen hanging in Italian grocery and fancy delicatessen stores. Scamorze has a delicate nutty flavor and a glossy, golden yellow skin. It may be eaten at the end of meals in pieces and also in some pasta dishes, best when fresh. In Italy there are some farms where Scamorze cheese is still made from goat's milk by the traditional methods.

Fusilli with Creamy Gorgonzola Sauce

A good reason for using gorgonzola in cooking, in addition to its good taste, is its ability to melt smoothly. This is an excellent sauce for fusilli and other pasta. Try it with the colored pastas too.

1. In a saucepan, combine the melted butter and gorgonzola. Stir until the cheese is melted.

2. Add the half and half, tomato purée, walnut halves, and cumin seed. Keep over very low heat or set aside until pasta is cooked.

3. Cook the fusilli until *al dente,* drain, and return to the pot in which they cooked. Add the parmesan cheese, cream sauce, and tomato cubes. Toss well and serve warm or lukewarm.

SERVES 4

INGREDIENTS
½ cup butter, melted
¼ pound gorgonzola
1 cup half and half
¼ cup tomato purée (not tomato paste)
¾ cup walnut halves
½ teaspoon cumin seed
1 pound fusilli
1 cup freshly grated parmesan cheese
1 large ripe tomato, peeled, seeded, and sliced fine, then cubed
salt
freshly ground black pepper

VARIATION
Use 1 pound rotelle (pasta wheels) in place of the fusilli; 12 basil leaves, chopped finely, instead of the cumin seed; and add 1 ounce of brandy (optional) to cheese sauce as soon as gorgonzola has melted.

WINE
A fiano di Avellino or a vernaccia di San Gimignano, both white wines with character

Vermicelli with Provolone

This simple but most tasty recipe I learned from the family of a friend in Genoa. We stopped in the market one bright day and admired the long tubes of yellow cheese, almost a yard long, 5 of them hanging from cords outside a cheese store. Of course, we bought some and hurried home to create a pasta dish. Provolone is a nutty cheese with a marvelous flavor.

1. Place the melted butter in a warm bowl.

2. Cook the vermicelli *al dente.* They will cook quickly, so test them for doneness every few seconds. Drain well and place in the bowl with the butter; using wooden forks, toss lightly, but well. Add half the cheese, grind lots of fresh black pepper into the pasta, and toss gently again.

SERVES 4 TO 6

INGREDIENTS
¼ *pound butter, melted*
1 pound vermicelli
1 cup grated provolone cheese
freshly ground black pepper

3. Add the remaining cheese, more pepper, and toss again. Serve hot.

WINE
A barbacarlo or other red table wine

Layered Pasta with Three Cheeses

Smoked mozzarella is the accent here as it combines with ricotta and parmesan. This is a rich dish, but not overly so.

1. Cook the tagliolini in salted boiling water and drain. Return to the pot in which they were cooked and add 4 tablespoons of butter. Toss lightly until butter is melted. Add a liberal amount of black pepper and the parsley and toss again.

2. Place half the cooked noodles in a 9- or 10-inch casserole or baking dish with high sides. Spread the ricotta over the top and sprinkle half the parmesan cheese over the ricotta. Do *not* toss.

3. Add the remaining noodles. Pour chicken stock overall. Sprinkle on the remaining parmesan cheese and the mozzarella pieces.

SERVES 4

INGREDIENTS
1 pound tagliolini, preferably homemade
6 tablespoons butter, in ½-inch cubes
freshly ground black pepper
¼ cup finely chopped fresh parsley
1 pound ricotta
½ cup freshly grated parmesan cheese
2 cups rich chicken stock, heated
½ cup fresh smoked mozzarella, in ¼-inch cubes

Dot with the remaining 2 tablespoons of butter, cover with the casserole cover or foil, and bake for 10 minutes. Serve hot.

WINE
A vernaccia di San Gimignano, or other dry white wine

Pasta Shells with
Mascarpone Cheese and Walnuts

This is an exquisite dish when well prepared, but it is filling and rich so a little goes a long way.

1. In a heatproof serving dish, melt the butter and cheese. It must gently heat, not boil.

2. To this mixture, add the cooked pasta. Turn it round and round adding half the parmesan cheese. Add the walnuts and add

SERVES 3 TO 4

INGREDIENTS
4 tablespoons butter
6 ounces mascarpone cheese or double-creme
½ pound pasta shells, cooked and drained
½ cup freshly grated parmesan cheese
2 ounces shelled walnuts, chopped coarse
salt
freshly ground black pepper

salt to taste. Sprinkle liberally with pepper. Serve remaining parmesan cheese separately.

WINE
A vernaccia di Oristano or other dry white wine

Fettuccine with Ricotta Nut Sauce

Pinenuts and walnuts combine well with pasta. The sauce seems a little busy, but is easy to prepare and tastes delicious.

1. Preheat the oven to 325 degrees. Spread the walnuts and pinenuts in a roasting pan or pie plate and toast in oven for 3 to 4 minutes or until golden. Be sure not to overtoast or you will have a burnt taste. Put the nuts in a blender or a food processor with the steel blade, add 1 tablespoon of water, and blend at high speed until smooth. (If using a blender, process ½ cup at a time.) Transfer to a bowl and add the ricotta, sugar, and mint; combine well, then set aside.

2. In a medium saucepan, heat the olive oil and sauté the garlic for 1 minute. Add the tomatoes, and cook for 2 minutes longer. Add the wine and basil and cook for 10 minutes more. Add salt and pepper to taste. Add the ricotta

SERVES 4

INGREDIENTS
½ cup chopped walnuts
½ cup pinenuts (pignoli)
1 cup ricotta
½ teaspoon sugar
¼ cup finely chopped fresh mint leaves, or 1 tablespoon dried
2 tablespoons olive oil
1 clove garlic, chopped fine
2 large ripe tomatoes, cut up and put through a food mill; or 1 cup seeded and puréed canned Italian plum tomatoes
¼ cup dry white wine or dry vermouth
1 tablespoon chopped fresh basil, or 1 teaspoon dried
salt and freshly ground black pepper
½ pound fettuccine or spaghettini
2 tablespoons butter
½ cup freshly grated romano or parmesan cheese

and nut mixture to the tomato sauce and heat until hot.

3. Cook the fettuccine until *al dente*. Drain and return to the pot in which it cooked. Add butter and mix until butter is melted. Add half the cheese and mix again. Add the ricotta nut sauce and toss well. Serve on individual plates, on a large platter or in a big bowl. Add remaining cheese and serve.

WINE
A tocai or other dry, medium-bodied white wine

Whole-Wheat Pasta with Ricotta

1. In a large skillet, heat the butter and olive oil until melted and combined. Add the garlic and sauté until pale. Do not brown the garlic.

2. Add the milk, cream, salt, and red pepper flakes. Heat the mixture to just *below* the boiling point. Then add the ricotta and half the parmesan cheese and blend well with a wire whisk until the mixture is creamy. Set aside but keep warm.

SERVES 4

INGREDIENTS
2 tablespoons butter
1 tablespoon olive oil
1 clove garlic, chopped fine
¼ cup milk
¼ cup heavy cream
1 teaspoon salt
⅛ teaspoon red pepper flakes
1 pound skim-milk ricotta
1 cup grated parmesan cheese
*1 pound whole-wheat
    spaghetti or fettuccine*
*2 tablespoons finely chopped
    parsley*

3. Cook the pasta until *al dente* and drain well. Place in a heated serving bowl and add the ricotta mixture. Toss lightly but well. Sprinkle the remaining ½ cup parmesan cheese and the parsley overall. Serve immediately.

WINE
An orvieto classico

Potato Gnocchi with Fontina

These gnocchi are made with potatoes and accented with fontina cheese and butter.

1. Preheat oven to 350 degrees, then bake the potatoes for 1 hour. Skin the potatoes and put them through a food mill or mash them. Set the mashed potatoes aside.

2. In a large bowl, mix the egg yolks, salt, nutmeg, and ½ cup of grated cheese; blend well. Add the mashed potatoes, then add the flour, a little at a time, until a dough forms and holds together. The dough should be soft but firm enough to roll.

3. On a floured board, roll small amounts of dough into small 1½-inch thick cylinders; cut each cylinder into ½-inch pieces. Take each piece and press it (and roll it) against a cheese grater. This gives the gnocchi a nice design and texture.

SERVES 6

INGREDIENTS
5 Idaho potatoes
2 egg yolks, at room temperature
¼ teaspoon salt
¼ teaspoon grated nutmeg
1 cup freshly grated parmesan, romano, or locatelli cheese
1½ cups all-purpose flour
¼ cup plus 2 tablespoons butter
¼ pound fontina cheese, sliced thin
2 cups Tomato Sauce (page 35), heated (optional)

4. Drop the gnocchi gently into 4 quarts of boiling salted water, and cook for 5 minutes or until they rise to the surface. With a slotted spoon, drain and transfer to a kitchen towel. Put them in an ovenproof dish.

5. Preheat the broiler. In a skillet or small saucepan, heat butter until brown and then pour over gnocchis. Add remaining ½ cup parmesan cheese, add fontina slices, and place on piping hot gnocchi. Run under the broiler for 1 or 2 minutes until fontina is melted and begins to brown. Gnocchi should be 6 inches or less from broiling unit. If desired, serve with tomato sauce on the side.

WINE
A verdicchio or other light, crisp white wine

Cheese and Spinach Dumplings

We can't explain why in the heavenly city of Florence there should be a pasta dish called Strozzapreti alla Fiorentina, *but there is.* Strozzapreti *means "it strangles priests." Why this should be so, in a Roman Catholic country, is baffling to us, but we can remember our father using the expression for this dish. In fact, this expression is used for other dishes in other provinces as well.*

1. Remove stems from spinach and wash leaves carefully to remove all sand. Bring spinach to a boil in salted water and drain immediately. Chop very fine.

2. In a bowl mix the spinach, ricotta, egg yolks, ½ cup of the parmesan cheese, salt, and spice mixture to a very smooth paste.

3. Put the flour on a large flat plate. Flour the palms of both your hands. Use a tablespoon and spoon out a ball of the ricotta mixture and roll it between your

SERVES 4 TO 6

INGREDIENTS

1 pound fresh spinach
1½ cups ricotta
4 egg yolks
1½ cups freshly grated parmesan cheese
¼ teaspoon salt
¼ teaspoon mixed black pepper, nutmeg, cloves, and ginger
1 cup all-purpose flour
2 cups hot beef stock
4 tablespoons butter

floured hands into oval-shaped balls, about 1½ inches long and 1 inch wide. Repeat this process until the mixture is used up. Be sure your hands are always floured.

4. Bring about 3 quarts of water with 1 tablespoon salt to a boil. Carefully add the dumplings, 1 at a time. Do not add too many to the pot at any one time or they will stick together. As soon as each ricotta ball rises to the top, remove it and drain well by placing on a cotton or linen towel. Put dumplings on a serving platter and pour the beef stock overall. Sprinkle with ½ cup of parmesan cheese, dot with small pieces of butter, and gently toss. Pass the remaining parmesan cheese.

WINE
A verdicchio or other dry, medium-bodied white wine

PASTA WITH VEGETABLES

*I*f we had to choose one family of foods to live with for the rest of our lives, we would choose vegetables. There are so many vegetables and so many ways to cook them. Moreover, we can't think of more beautiful things to look at. What can compare with the shape, color, or gleam of a bright red tomato? a smooth-as-silk, deep purple eggplant? the pure white mound of a mushroom? a bunch of carrots, with their fernlike ends? lacy celery hearts? fresh, pale green dandelion leaves? a majestic artichoke? a family of garlic cloves? the regal leek? the beauty and mystery of the inner rings of an onion?

When Italians prepare a dish of meat, chicken, or game they rarely serve an accompaniment other than small potatoes and a salad. Vegetables are usually presented as a separate dish, usually as a first course; for example, a famous Roman dish is *Carciofi alla Giudea,* an artichoke fried whole in oil. However, many vegetables are used with pasta and sometimes the vegetable even forms the pasta itself, as with pasta verde, made with spinach. Other times the vegetable serves as part of the filling for a stuffed pasta—for example, spinach and mushrooms in tortellini. In spite of the customary sauces of butter and cream, olive oil and garlic, and tomato with basil, it is becoming popular these days to combine fresh vegetables and pasta. These primavera pasta dishes combine many vegetables with pastas: mushrooms, broccoli, peas, and zucchini to name just a few.

When shopping, remember that fresh vegetables should always have a crisp bright color with no blemishes. Artichokes should be fresh (when cut, the stem is white and somewhat juicy). Asparagus tips should be tightly closed, stems crisp and moist. Greens should be attached to beets and carrots. Broccoli should have firm, dark leaves with compact bud clusters and no yellow in the florets. Cauliflower should be creamy white and closely knit. Always choose small to medium firm eggplants that are relatively heavy and look for those with their caplike bracts and stem firmly attached. Mushroom caps should be firmly curled, not flared open; it is better to buy them loose, though they may cost a little more. Peas are best in the pod, but pods should be smooth and shiny and free of wrinkles. Potatoes should not have a musty odor or a green tinge. Spinach is best bought in bundles; leaves should be a rich forest green, preferably small and straight. Tomatoes are best when ripened on the vine; often during the winter months the canned Italian plum tomatoes are more flavorful than so-called fresh ones. Zucchini should be small, about 1 inch thick and 5 to 6 inches long. Avoid any that are pale or whose skin is not taut.

To keep vegetables green while cooking, drop them into rapidly boiling water. Allow the water to come to a second boil and continue boiling until barely tender. Do not cover. Drain immediately.

Artichokes with Spinach Pasta

The delicate flavor of artichokes is brought out in this recipe.

1. Select artichokes that are young and fresh. Cut off the stems so that bottoms are flush, then lay artichokes on their sides. Cut off the top third and then cut each into quarters. Use a sharp knife to remove the furry "choke" just above the bottom. Dip the artichokes in a bowl of cool water in which you have 1 or 2 tablespoons of lemon juice. This will prevent discoloration as you trim the remaining artichokes.

2. In a large skillet, heat 2 tablespoons of the oil and sauté the artichoke quarters until they are tender. Remove them from the heat, transfer to a small bowl, set aside, and keep warm.

3. Cook the spinach spaghetti until *al dente.*

4. While the spaghetti is cooking, heat the remaining 4 table-

SERVES 4

INGREDIENTS

6 tablespoons butter
1 tablespoon olive oil
6 fresh artichoke hearts
½ pound spinach spaghetti
1 clove garlic, finely chopped
1¼ cups heavy cream
½ cup early peas, cooked
½ cup freshly grated
*   parmesan cheese*

spoons of butter in the same skillet in which the artichokes were sautéed. When melted, add the garlic and sauté until they just begin to color. Add the cream and heat just to the boiling point.

5. Drain the spaghetti and return it to the pan in which it cooked. Pour the sauce into the spaghetti and toss lightly. Use a rubber spatula to transfer all of this sauce into the pasta pan. Add the peas and toss lightly.

6. Transfer the spaghetti to individual plates or to 1 large bowl or platter. Sprinkle the pasta with parmesan cheese. Top with the artichoke hearts, and serve.

NOTE

You could substitute frozen artichokes. Avoid canned or bottled artichokes; they will taste somewhat "tinny."

WINE

A pinot grigio or another light, dry white wine

Artichoke Hearts and Carrots with Spaghettini

This light pasta dish is colorful and can be a whole meal, served with a green salad.

1. In a medium pan over medium heat, heat 1 tablespoon of butter and 2 tablespoons of oil. When the butter and oil are hot, add the garlic and shallots. Sauté briefly, about 2 minutes. Add remaining ½ cup of oil, lower the heat, and let the oil get hot. Turn the heat off, and set pan aside.

2. In another medium pan put about 1½ inches of water and place in a steamer. Let the water come to a fast boil and add the carrots. Cover the pot and steam the carrots for 2 minutes. Set aside.

3. If using frozen artichoke hearts, place the artichokes in a saucepan with ½ cup of water and 1 teaspoon of salt. Cover the pan and let the artichokes come to a fast boil. Lower the heat and simmer for about 12 minutes or until

SERVES 6

INGREDIENTS

5 tablespoons butter
½ cup and 2 tablespoons olive oil
4 cloves garlic, minced
6 shallots, minced
4 carrots, scraped, washed, and cut into thin strips (¼ by 2 inches)
6 fresh artichokes, cooked; or 2 packages (9 ounces each) frozen artichoke hearts—do not use canned or jarred
1 pound whole-wheat spaghettini
1 teaspoon salt
¼ to ½ cup freshly grated romano cheese
½ teaspoon red pepper flakes

very tender. Drain; if the artichoke hearts are large, cut them in half. Return to the same pan in which they cooked and add 2 tablespoons of butter. Set aside.

4. Cook the pasta until *al dente*. Drain, but leave a little water in the bottom of the pan. Return the pasta to the pan in which it cooked. Add 2 tablespoons of butter and toss quickly. Add the oil mixture and toss with the pasta. Adjust salt seasoning, if necessary.

5. Have ready a large oval platter. Transfer the pasta to it. Sprinkle some of the cheese on top. Arrange the vegetables around and sprinkle the red pepper flakes *only* on the artichoke hearts. Serve immediately and pass more cheese.

WINE
A light red, such as Riviera del Garda Rosso

Fresh Broccoli with Spinach Fusilli

Broccoli has a long history. It has always been a favorite among gourmets and was highly esteemed by the Romans. Drusas, son on the emperor Tiberius, one day ate so much broccoli that his father chided him for his greediness which, considering the extraordinary eating habits of wealthy Romans in those times, makes one wonder how much broccoli the young man did in fact consume.

1. In a medium skillet, heat the oil and sauté the onion and garlic for 2 minutes. Add the carrot and capers and cook 1 minute longer.

2. Add the beef stock and the red pepper flakes. Cook slowly for about 5 minutes. Add salt to taste and set aside for a few minutes.

SERVES 4

INGREDIENTS

1/4 cup olive oil
1 small onion, chopped fine
1 large clove garlic, chopped fine
1 small carrot, chopped fine
1 teaspoon drained capers
3/4 cup beef stock
1/4 teaspoon red pepper flakes
salt
1/2 bunch fresh broccoli, washed, trimmed and cut into 1-inch lengths
1/2 pound spinach fusilli
1/2 cup freshly grated romano cheese

3. In a medium pan, add 4 or 5 cups of water and let it come to a fast boil. Add the broccoli and cook for 5 minutes. They should be tender, yet firm to the bite. Drain and set aside.

4. Cook the spinach fusilli until *al dente.* Drain and return to the pan in which they cooked. Add the broccoli sauce to the pasta. Also add half the cheese. Mix well. Serve in individual plates or in a large bowl or serving platter. Add the remaining cheese on top.

WINE
A valpolicella or other dry, medium-bodied red wine

On the following pages: Thin Spaghetti with a Rich Seafood Sauce (recipe on page 122); Pasta Rustica (recipe on page 135); Pasta Primavera Mold (recipe on page 130); Pasta with Chicken, Rosemary, and Basil (recipe on page 106).

Pasta with Cauliflower and Cacciocavallo

Cauliflower combines well with pasta; you'll be pleasantly surprised.

1. Preheat the oven to 350 degrees. Remove all the leaves from the cauliflower and scoop out most of the stalk. Don't cut too deeply, or you'll end up with florets instead. Cook the full head by boiling it in water with lemon juice and salt for 8 to 10 minutes. The cauliflower should be firm. Remove it from the liquid, cool, and cut it in small florets, about 1 inch in size.

2. Put the olive oil in a baking pan. Add the cauliflower, garlic, parsley, and salt and pepper to taste and toss well. Bake in moderate oven for about 6 minutes, then remove this from the oven and sprinkle with the cheese and 3 tablespoons of butter while hot.

SERVES 4

INGREDIENTS

1 medium cauliflower
juice of 1 lemon
1 tablespoon salt
½ cup extra-virgin olive oil
½ teaspoon chopped garlic
1 tablespoon chopped fresh parsley
salt
freshly ground black pepper
¾ pound cacciocavallo cheese, coarsely ground in a food mill
6 tablespoons butter
1 pound cavatelli, penne, pennette, mostaciolle, or any short pasta
red pepper flakes to taste

3. Meanwhile, cook the pasta until *al dente*. Drain well and return to the pan in which it cooked. Toss with remaining 3 tablespoons butter. Add the cauliflower mixture, being sure to transfer all the butter and oil left in the baking pan (use a rubber spatula). Toss the pasta, cauliflower, and butter and oil until well mixed. Serve immediately in individual bowls or in a large bowl or platter with crushed red pepper.

WINE
A rubesco riserva or other Italian red such as brunello di Montalcino

Eggplant and Fresh Tagliatelle

In addition to a good taste, this sauce is a practical one for it can be made ahead of time, eggplant and all, by as much as several days.

1. Wash or wipe clean the eggplant. Remove the ends; peel if large, but don't fret if some of its purple skin remains. Slice the eggplant as thinly as you can. Set the slices in a colander, add salt, and allow to drain for at least 30 minutes.

2. Pour about ½ inch of vegetable oil in a large skillet and turn the heat to high. When the oil is sizzling, dry enough eggplant slices to fit into the skillet at one time and fry them to a golden color on both sides. Transfer to paper toweling and repeat procedure until all the eggplant slices are fried.

3. In a medium saucepan, heat the olive oil and sauté the garlic over moderate heat just until it

SERVES 4 TO 6

INGREDIENTS
1 eggplant, about 1 pound
salt
vegetable oil for sautéeing
3 tablespoons olive oil
3 small or 2 large cloves
garlic, chopped fine
2 tablespoons finely chopped
fresh parsley
2 cups puréed canned Italian
plum tomatoes
⅛ teaspoon red pepper flakes
1 pound freshly made
tagliatelle

NOTE
Generally this dish is not served with grated cheese, but you be your own judge. The pasta may be served in individual bowls with sauce spooned on top of each serving.

begins to color lightly. Add the parsley, tomato purée, hot pepper flakes, and salt to taste. Stir to combine ingredients and cook uncovered over low heat for about 25 minutes or until the tomatoes are separated from the oil and turn to sauce. When the sauce is ready, add the eggplant and cook for 2 or 3 minutes more. Adjust salt seasoning and keep the sauce warm, but cook no further.

4. Cook the tagliatelle, drain, and return to the pan in which they cooked. Add a small quantity of the sauce. Toss lightly with 1 or 2 wooden forks. Transfer to a large warm bowl and add the rest of the sauce quickly. Mix again and serve immediately.

WINE
A montepulciano d'Abruzzo or other dry red wine

Fusilli with Eggplant and Tomatoes

Known for thousands of years as the mala insana (raging apple), eggplant was always soaked in salt and cold water to remove its "insanity." We salt and drain it, not because we fear its poisonous drippings, but because we want it to be less bitter.

1. Put the dried mushrooms in a small bowl, cover them with lukewarm water, and let stand for about 30 minutes. Meanwhile, spread eggplant out on paper towels, sprinkle with salt, and let drain for 30 minutes.

2. In a large skillet, heat the olive oil, add the chili pepper, and cook until the pepper becomes crisp. Remove and transfer to a paper towel.

3. In the same skillet, sauté the eggplant cubes on all sides for about 15 minutes. Stir them frequently, and don't be alarmed at how much oil they absorb. Add the garlic pieces, and sauté for 2 minutes longer.

SERVES 4 TO 6

INGREDIENTS
½ cup porcini (dried mushrooms)
1 medium eggplant, diced
½ cup olive oil
1 whole dried chili pepper
1 clove garlic, chopped fine
4 large fresh tomatoes, peeled and diced; or 2 cups chopped canned Italian plum tomatoes with some liquid
2 tablespoons chopped fresh parsley, or 2 teaspoons dried
1 tablespoon chopped fresh basil, or 1 teaspoon dried
salt
freshly ground black pepper
1 pound fusilli
2 tablespoons butter, softened
6 tablespoons freshly grated parmesan cheese

4. Add the tomatoes, parsley, basil, and salt and pepper to taste. Crush chili pepper, discard the seeds, and add pepper to skillet.

5. Drain the mushrooms, and cut them into small pieces. Add them to the skillet. Bring this mixture to a boil, lower the heat, and cook for 30 minutes, or until eggplant cubes are tender. Check sauce for seasoning, and add salt and pepper if needed.

6. While the eggplant is cooking, cook the fusilli until *al dente*. Drain and return to the pan in which they were cooked. Add butter, and stir well. Add the sauce and combine well. Serve on individual plates or in 1 large bowl or serving platter. Serve with parmesan cheese.

WINE
A dolcetto or other dry, medium-bodied red wine

Fettuccine with Mushrooms and Prosciutto

Fettuccine with mushrooms and prosciutto is a wonderful combination of flavors and textures. Classic variations of this dish exist all over northern Italy; we think this one is special and was given to us by friends in Milan.

1. Heat olive oil and butter in a large skillet and when bubbling, add mushrooms and cook until they are lightly browned, approximately 10 minutes.

2. To the skillet add the prosciutto bits, tomatoes, nutmeg, sage, and cream. Cook over high heat for 4 or 5 minutes until sauce is somewhat thickened. Remove from heat and set aside.

3. Cook fettuccine until *al dente,* drain, and return to pot in which they cooked. Add salt and pepper to taste, then add the

SERVES 4 TO 6

INGREDIENTS
3 tablespoons olive oil
3 tablespoons butter
1 pound fresh mushrooms, trimmed and sliced thin
½ pound prosciutto, cut in bits
2 large ripe tomatoes, peeled, seeded, and chopped into ½-inch cubes; or ½ cup tomatoe purée
¼ teaspoon ground nutmeg
2 fresh sage leaves, chopped fine; or 1 teaspoon dried sage leaves, rubbed between your hands
1 cup heavy cream
1 pound fettuccine
salt
freshly ground black pepper
1 cup freshly grated parmesan cheese
½ cup finely chopped flat parsley

sauce and half the parmesan. Toss well and transfer quickly to serving bowl or platter or to individual serving plates. Add the remaining parmesan cheese and fresh parsley to either the single large platter or individual plates and serve immediately.

VARIATION
Toast ⅔ cup of pinenuts, walnuts, almonds, or hazelnuts and sprinkle on top just before serving.

WINE
An etna blanco superiore or other dry and well-balanced white wine

Porcini and Tomatoes with Spinach Pasta

This is a heavier pasta dish, but the dried mushrooms add abundant flavor for just as tasty a combination.

1. Soak the mushrooms in a cup of warm water for about 30 minutes. Arrange cheesecloth or paper toweling over a small bowl and place a strainer over this. Pour mushrooms and liquid into strainer allowing liquid to clear itself through cheesecloth or toweling. Run some cool water over mushrooms in strainer, drain well, and chop them if larger than ½ inch in size. Reserve liquid.

2. In a large skillet or medium saucepan heat the oil and butter. When they bubble, add the onion and sauté for 3 minutes or so until it begins to turn color. Add the prosciutto and sauté another 2 minutes. Add the tomatoes, salt, pepper, mushrooms, and mushroom liquid, and cook *un*covered

SERVES 5 TO 6

INGREDIENTS

1 ounce porcini (dried mushrooms)
2 tablespoons olive oil
4 tablespoons butter
½ onion, peeled and chopped fine
2 tablespoons prosciutto cubes, ¼ inch wide
4 ripe medium tomatoes, peeled, seeded, and chopped in ½-inch cubes; or 2 cups puréed canned Italian plum tomatoes
½ teaspoon salt
freshly ground black pepper
1 pound spinach fusilli
1 to 2 cups freshly grated parmesan cheese

at a bare simmer for 40 minutes. Stir every 10 minutes or so and be sure to maintain a simmer and not a boil.

3. Cook the pasta until *al dente,* drain well, and return to the pot in which it cooked. Pour the sauce over the pasta, combine well, and serve as soon as you can. Pass the parmesan cheese and allow each person to add the cheese to his or her serving of pasta.

WINE
A buttafuoco or other medium-bodied red wine

Peas with Pasta Shells

Our grandmother Nonna had a market test for peas: the fingernail press. She would hold a pea pod in her hand and press a cut into the pod with the fingernail of her thumb or index finger. If she didn't buy a pound or 2 of fresh peas, it was because no moisture had appeared in the cut. But, if the cut was moist, the peas were fresh and the sale was consummated.

1. Steam or cook the peas in very little water for 5 to 7 minutes. (If you have very young fresh peas, melt 1 tablespoon of butter in a pan and add peas; cover with several lettuce leaves then cover pan and cook slowly until tender.) Set aside.

2. In a 2-quart saucepan, heat the oil and sauté the onion until it begins to soften and turn color. Add the garlic, and cook 2 minutes longer. Add the tomatoes, and cook slowly for 10 minutes.

SERVES 4

INGREDIENTS

3 cups fresh or frozen peas
3 tablespoons olive oil
1 large onion, chopped fine
1 large garlic clove, chopped fine
4 fresh tomatoes, peeled and chopped coarse; or 2 cups coarsely chopped canned Italian plum tomatoes with some liquid
½ pound pasta shells, preferably occhi di lupo ("eyes of the wolf") Cirio brand, made and packaged in Naples; or 1-inch macaroni shells manufactured domestically
10 leaves fresh basil, washed, dried, and chopped fine
salt
freshly ground black pepper
½ cup freshly grated parmesan cheese

3. While the tomatoes are cooking, cook the pasta and drain. When the tomatoes have cooked 10 minutes, add the peas and the pasta. Then add the basil and salt and pepper to taste, and bring to a boil. Remove from the heat, and serve immediately with the freshly grated parmesan cheese in a separate bowl.

NOTE
Instead of green peas, use equal amounts of baby lima beans or black-eyed peas.

WINE
A white sauvignon or other dry white wine

Pasta with Green Peas, Basil, and Scallions

This is a great summertime dish if you can pick fresh peas, scallions, and basil from your garden. It is delicious cooked with freshly made fettuccine or other egg noodles.

1. If using fresh peas, parboil and drain. If using frozen, boil to thaw and drain.

2. Heat the butter in a large skillet and add the vermouth and scallions. Cook for about 10 minutes until scallions turn soft and the vermouth thickens and deglazes the pan.

SERVES 4

INGREDIENTS

2 cups fresh or frozen green peas
2 tablespoons butter
¼ cup dry vermouth
½ cup chopped fresh scallions, including tender green parts
2 tablespoons finely chopped fresh basil, or 1 teaspoon dried
½ pound freshly made pasta
salt
freshly ground black pepper

3. Add the peas and basil, turn the heat to high for 2 minutes, and pour immediately over pasta. Toss well and serve.

WINE
A bardolino or other dry, light red wine

Spinach, Mushrooms, and Cream with Spaghetti

This is one of the best pasta preparations in this book. Mushrooms and cream, accented by lemon, make this special.

1. Cook the spinach in boiling, salted water until it is tender. Drain well, and set aside.

2. Wipe the mushrooms with damp kitchen toweling and cut off stem ends. Slice thin, add lemon juice, and mix well.

3. Melt the butter in a skillet, and add the garlic and marsala. Cook for 3 minutes, then add the mushrooms. Cook an additional 5 minutes, then add the cream and bring the mixture to a boil. Add some salt, then pepper liberally. Remove from heat.

SERVES 2 TO 4

INGREDIENTS
4 cups shredded fresh spinach leaves
½ pound fresh mushrooms
juice of 1 lemon
4 tablespoons butter
1 clove garlic, chopped fine
2 tablespoons marsala
1 cup heavy cream
salt
freshly ground black pepper
½ pound spaghetti
4 heaping tablespoons grated parmesan cheese

4. Cook the spaghetti (or other pasta) until *al dente*. Drain and return it to the pot in which it was cooked. Add first the cooked spinach and then the mushroom mixture to the pasta. Put the sauced spaghetti in individual serving plates, and top each with parmesan cheese.

WINE
A Friuli pinot blanco or other light white wine

Penne with Tomatoes, Pancetta, and Red Pepper

The pancetta gives this light sauce a unique flavor.

1. In a large skillet, heat the butter and vegetable oil (do not use olive oil—pancetta renders its own special fat and vegetable oil is better combined with it) and sauté the pancetta pieces until they begin to brown, about 4 minutes.

2. Add the onion pieces and cook for 4 more minutes over low to medium heat until the onion becomes opaque and pale yellow.

3. Add the tomatoes, pepper flakes, and salt. Cook uncovered at a lower simmer for 20 minutes, or until the oil and pancetta fat separate from the tomatoes; you will be able to see this quite clearly. Remove from the heat and set aside.

SERVES 4 TO 6

INGREDIENTS
3 tablespoons butter
2 tablespoons vegetable oil
¼-inch-thick slice pancetta roll, unrolled and diced into ¼-inch pieces
¾ cup finely chopped onion
4 ripe medium tomatoes, peeled, seeded, and chopped into ½-inch cubes; or 2 cups seeded and chopped canned Italian plum tomatoes
¼ teaspoon red pepper flakes
1½ teaspoons salt
1 pound penne
4 tablespoons freshly grated parmesan cheese
1 tablespoon chopped fresh parsley

4. Cook the penne until *al dente*. Drain and transfer them to the pot in which they cooked. Add one-third of the sauce and mix well. Transfer the pasta to a large serving bowl or platter or to individual plates and pour remaining sauce overall or divide among individual portions. Sprinkle cheese overall or 1 tablespoon per serving. Dot with parsley bits.

WINE
A sangiouese di Romagna or other dry red wine

Pasta in Truffled Cream Sauce

White truffles, tartufi bianchi, *are really light brown in color. They grow in Tuscany, in Romagna, and in Piedmont. Hunted out by trained dogs in a season lasting from October through March, their scent is much more powerful than black truffles. They are frightfully expensive when available in this country, and for this reason, the following pasta preparation uses either black or white truffles.*

1. Combine the stock, vermouth, and, if using canned black truffles, any juice you have from the can or bottle. Bring to a boil, lower heat, and simmer for 15 minutes. Add truffles to the stock and set aside.

2. In a skillet, heat 4 tablespoons of butter and sauté the mushroom slices until they are heated through; they should be on the raw side. Set aside.

SERVES 6

INGREDIENTS

3½ cups rich beef, veal, or chicken stock
½ cup dry vermouth
3 or 4 small black truffles, or 1 white truffle, sliced thin and slivered
8 tablespoons butter
1 pound fresh mushrooms, trimmed and sliced thin
2 cups heavy cream
salt
freshly ground black pepper
1½ pounds freshly made pasta (fettuccine or tagliatelle)
2 cups freshly grated parmesan cheese
¾ cup thinly sliced scallions

3. In a saucepan, heat the cream to the boiling point, season with salt and pepper, then use a rubber spatula to gather all the butter and mushrooms as you transfer them to the cream.

4. Cook the pasta, drain it, and return it to the pot in which it cooked. Add the remaining butter and toss the pasta quickly. Add the truffle mixture, the mushrooms and cream, and half the parmesan cheese.

5. Divide pasta among 6 or 8 plates or put all into one large platter. Sprinkle the scallions and the remaining parmesan cheese overall. This is one pasta dish to serve with soup spoons; not to eat the pasta, but to spoon up any remaining sauce.

WINE
A donnaz from the Val d'Aosta, or other full-bodied red wine

Zucchini and Farfalloni

A wonderful pasta combination of big butterflies with creamy zucchini. Big butterflies may be something in one's fantasy, but served this way, they are part of the real world.

1. In a small bowl combine flour and milk and set aside.

2. In a medium skillet pour enough vegetable or corn oil to come up the skillet ½ inch. Over medium heat, heat the oil until it just begins to bubble. Add about one-fourth of the zucchini pieces and sauté until lightly browned. With a slotted spoon, transfer the zucchini to paper towels. Repeat until all the zucchini are sautéed in this way.

3. In a large skillet add the olive oil and 2 tablespoons butter and bring to the bubbly stage over medium-high heat. When the butter bubbles, reduce heat to low and slowly add the zucchini and stir gently several times. Add

SERVES 4

INGREDIENTS
1 teaspoon all-purpose flour
⅓ cup milk
vegetable or corn oil
1 pound zucchini, trimmed and cut into julienne pieces
3 tablespoons olive oil
3 tablespoons butter
¾ cup finely chopped fresh basil
½ teaspoon salt
1 egg yolk, lightly beaten
½ cup freshly grated romano cheese
½ cup freshly grated parmesan cheese
½ pound farfalloni (big butterflies)

the basil and salt and continue cooking only until the zucchini is heated through. Immediately remove from the heat and stir in the remaining butter.

4. Quickly beat the egg yolk into the zucchini mixture and stir in both cheeses. Check seasoning and adjust if necessary.

5. Cook the big butterflies to the *al dente* stage, drain well, and return to the pot in which they cooked. Add the sauce and toss lightly, but thoroughly. Serve immediately in individual plates or in a large bowl or a single large platter.

WINE
A dry white wine from Avellino, perhaps lachrima christi

Pasta Primavera

Pasta Primavera means "springtime pasta," originated in New York at Le Cirque. The primavera is a combination of parboiled and then sautéed fresh vegetables. Primavera, which uses the youngest of fresh spring produce, invites innovation—so characteristic of the Italian kitchen, especially with its pasta cookery. This preparation lists many ingredients and, on the surface, seems complicated. Actually it is quite simple, if done in 3 steps: prepare and cook the vegetables; prepare a tomato sauce; toast the pinenuts, cook the pasta, and assemble all the ingredients.

1. Cook the zucchini, asparagus, beans, peas, broccoli, and snow peas separately. Keep them *al dente*—do not overcook them as you will cook them again later when you sauté them. Drain each green vegetable and dry in kitchen toweling. Combine all green vegetables in a large bowl and set aside.

SERVES 6

INGREDIENTS

2 very small zucchini, trimmed and sliced ¼-inch thick
6 asparagus spears, trimmed and cut into 1-inch lengths
1 cup sliced green beans, approximately 1 inch long
½ cup fresh or frozen peas
1 bunch broccoli, washed, trimmed and cut into 1-inch florets
¾ cup fresh snow peas, ends removed and cut on bias into 1-inch pieces
2 tablespoons olive oil
2 tablespoons butter
2 cloves garlic, finely chopped
1 cup sliced fresh mushrooms
⅓ cup finely chopped fresh parsley
½ teaspoon dried red pepper flakes

2. In a large skillet, or saucepan, heat the olive oil and butter and sauté the garlic until it just begins to turn color. Add the mushrooms and sauté for 2 or 3 minutes, then add the parsley and red pepper flakes. Cook another minute. Add all the green vegetables and sauté for about 5 minutes stirring frequently, but gently.

3. Meanwhile, in another large skillet, heat the oil and butter for the tomato sauce and cook the garlic until it just turns color. Add the basil and tomatoes and cook for 5 minutes. Set aside.

4. Cook the pasta until *al dente,* drain, and return it to the pot in which it cooked. Add the butter and toss lightly.

5. Add the cream and chicken stock. Toss the pasta some more. Add half the vegetable mixture, then the cheese, and toss again.

6. Transfer all the pasta to a large serving platter, add the remaining vegetables, pour tomato sauce overall, but let some of the green vegetables show through. Dot with toasted pinenuts and serve immediately.

1 teaspoon salt
freshly ground black pepper
1 pound thin pasta
   (vermicelli, spaghettini,
   spaghetti)
3 tablespoons butter, softened
½ cup heavy cream, heated
½ cup chicken stock, heated
1 cup freshly grated parmesan
   cheese
½ cup toasted pinenuts

TOMATO SAUCE
⅓ cup olive oil
4 tablespoons butter
3 cloves garlic, finely chopped
¼ cup freshly chopped basil,
   or 1 teaspoon dried
3 cups canned Italian plum
   tomatoes, including some
   juice, put through a food
   mill

NOTE
If the pasta is too dry, add a little more chicken stock and cream, but the pasta should not be in a liquidy sauce.

WINE
A dolcetto from Piedmont or other intensely fruity, soft-bodied dry red wine

Rigatoni with Zucchini Slices

As versatile as the potato, the zucchini is a special vegetable because it combines so well with so many other foods, especially with pasta.

1. In a 1½- or 2-quart casserole or a saucepan that has a tight-fitting lid, heat 1 tablespoon of butter and the oil and allow it to get bubbly. Add the garlic and sauté 1 minute, then turn the heat off.

2. Arrange half the zucchini slices in the bottom of the pan, top with the onion slices, tomato, basil, sweet red pepper, salt and pepper to taste, and, if you wish, some red pepper flakes. Top with the remaining zucchini slices. Season with salt and pepper again. Add the chicken stock, cover tightly, let the zucchini come to a fast boil, and then simmer on very low heat for 15 minutes. If the zucchini is very fresh, it will take only 10 minutes,

SERVES 3 TO 4

INGREDIENTS

3 tablespoons butter
1 tablespoon olive oil
1 clove garlic, chopped fine
4 small zucchini, sliced thin
1 onion, sliced thin and circles separated
1 large ripe tomato, peeled, seeded, and cut into ½-inch cubes; or ½ cup chopped canned Italian plum tomatoes
2 tablespoons finely chopped fresh basil, or 1 tablespoon dried
1 small red bell pepper, diced
½ teaspoon hot red pepper flakes (optional)
salt
freshly ground black pepper
½ cup chicken stock
½ cup coarsely grated freshly grated asiago cheese
½ pound rigatoni or shells

so check the cooking every couple of minutes. When the zucchini are *al dente,* sprinkle one-fourth of the cheese overall and set aside. This dish can be cooked 1 or 2 hours before serving and reheated quickly.

3. Cook the rigatoni until *al dente.* Drain well and return the pasta to the pot in which it cooked. Add the remaining 2 tablespoons of butter and mix. Add the remaining cheese and mix well. Serve in individual bowls. Put the pasta in the bottom of each bowl and spoon the zucchini mixture on top with some of its juice. Sprinkle more cheese on each serving.

WINE
A lacrimarosa—a rosé wine from Campania, South of Italy

PASTA WITH POULTRY, MEAT, OR FISH

I talians are not big meat eaters and meat in itself is not the primary food at the table. It is, as is chicken or fish, there only as part of an entire procession of foods where vegetables, pastas, and cheeses are equally important. With pasta, meats and fish play a role in creating sauces but again, they don't overwhelm or take away from the pasta or other ingredients.

In this chapter, chicken is joined with rosemary, basil, and pasta. Chicken innards are the basis for pasta sauces, for exciting uses for livers, gizzards, and hearts. Pork is the flavoring in sausages in marinara sauce, ham in the straw and hay pasta, and salami in coppa and eggs. Veal is used in a sauce with vegetables and tomatoes; and a pork roast, simmered in a tomato sauce, is featured also. Salt pork and pancetta, used in small quantities, are famous and excellent flavors in Italian pasta preparations; *spaghetti alla matriciana* is a well-known Roman dish that uses salt pork.

A recipe that uses pancetta in a pasta pie, or frittata, is utterly charming and delicious. This type of pasta dish is becoming the fair-haired child of the pasta world because it is easy to prepare, may be made ahead, can be served cool or at room temperature, and simply requires sliced fresh tomatoes or a green salad as an accompaniment.

Although the fish found in Italian waters are not available here, the good news is that much North American fish works well in creating the Italian tastes. Red snapper, halibut, squid, and striped bass, for example, can be used in these pasta dishes with great success.

The marinara sauce, a truly light and fresh tomato sauce (its meaning is "of the sea"), lends itself easily and well to sea sauces. Clam and lobster sauces have become traditional, and we've added a scallop sauce as well. We've used the clams, lobster, and scallops of this country in unusual and tasty sauces that capture the essence of Italian cooking. Lastly, imported Italian tuna has a divine taste, and it combines well with pasta and with anchovies and green peas.

Some of the popular Italian salamis and other prepared meats are available in the United States and since they create good flavors for pasta sauces, you should attempt to use them. Don't hesitate to substitute coppa for prosciutto, or mortadella too. Sopressata is especially tasty and can be used to accent a marinara sauce if you don't have sausages on hand.

COPPA OR CAPICOLLA: This is a delicious, dry, aired-cured salami made from seasoned pork shoulder butt. It is slowly cured to bring out a mellow taste, and its characteristic flavor is a bit more robust than prosciutto but just as tender. Many Italians love to make an entire meal of plain coppa with freshly baked bread, always with Italian wine of course. It is also excellent with fresh Italian cheeses such as mozzarella or ricotta, yet is also good with fontina or a young provolone.

Coppa is most often enjoyed in very thin slices. One variation is to cut the slices into thin strips (julienne) and add the strips to the pasta. It may also be cubed and added to pasta soups.

MORTADELLA SAUSAGE: This is often called bologna, and it is still made in Bologna, which has the reputation of making the best. A similar sausage is called *mortadelle,* served as an hors d'oeuvre. Mortadella has a smooth texture and delicate taste. Various cuts of pork are ground, boiled and larded, and put in casings as large as 16 to 18 inches (in Bologna only); in this country, they are usually in 6- and 8-inch sizes.

PANCETTA: Pancetta is like bacon (the same cut of pork) but it is not smoked. That is the main difference, although some claim pancetta

Opposite: Potato Gnocchi Roll (recipe on page 162). Following page: Farfalle Salad in Vermicelli Bird Nests (recipe on page 169).

is less greasy. Unless you are near an Italian specialty shop, you're not likely to find pancetta. It comes in casing like salami and will keep 3 weeks or so, tightly wrapped, in the refrigerator. The butcher can slice off any amount of the roll for you, so buy it that way. For example, if a recipe calls for a ¼-inch slice of pancetta, buy that exact amount and perhaps another slice to store for the next use.

PROSCIUTTO: Although prosciutto has been made for many, many years in Italy, it is possible to find an excellent prosciutto made in the United States. One brand we have found acceptable is by Citterio. They do not use spices, just sprinklings of pepper. Their aging program is unhurried; in fact, they say it takes an entire year. The significant characteristics of a good prosciutto are: a pleasing red color (look for *il colore rose*); a pleasing fragrance and flavor (smell *il profumo invitante*); a sweetness and natural taste of the prosciutto (taste it for *il sapore dolce e delicato*); the tenderness of the prosciutto itself (taste also for *la tennerezza eccezionale*). Before buying prosciutto, ask your butcher for a sample.

SOPRESSATA: These are small, coarse-grind salami, created well over a 100 years ago in the many farmhouses all over Italy. Long before electric grinders were available, the meat was meticulously chopped with a sharp knife, seasoned to the maker's personal taste, then hung up to be aged in time for special holidays such as Christmas and Easter. The seasoning is quite subtle: salt, pepper, and a touch of fresh garlic. It may be thinly sliced as an appetizer or snack; it combines well with crusty bread and a sturdy red Italian wine; it can be chopped fine as a marvelous flavoring in pasta dishes.

Opposite: Mussels with Green Pasta (recipe on page 117). Preceding page: Pasta Wheels in a Sweet-Sour Salad (recipe on page 170).

To this day there are selected food shops in many old Italian neighborhoods of large U.S. cities that continue this fine old-country tradition of making their own sopressata. However, much of what you'll find in the shops is manufactured by the firm Citterio, a company founded in Milano in 1878, but now with a branch in this country.

Pasta with Chicken, Rosemary, and Basil

This is a simple, light pasta dish, high-lighted with the special taste of rose-mary.

1. Combine the lemon juice and the chicken in a small bowl and let stand for 20 minutes.

2. Pat the chicken dry and then heat clarified butter in a skillet. Add chicken and sauté over high heat until brown on both sides— approximately 3 or 4 minutes on each side but more if the breasts are extra thick.

3. Add the olives, garlic, rosemary, basil, and salt and pepper to taste. Cover and cook 3 minutes.

4. Remove the chicken breasts and cut them in julienne strips. Set aside. Add 1 cup of stock to the skillet, and over high heat, boil liquid until it thickens and comes away from the pan.

5. Cook the pasta until *al dente,* drain, and return it to the

SERVES 4

INGREDIENTS
juice of ½ lemon
4 chicken breasts, boned and skin and fat removed
3 tablespoons clarified butter
6 oil-cured black olives, pitted and chopped fine
1 clove garlic
1½ teaspoons finely chopped fresh rosemary; or ½ teaspoon dried, rubbed in palms of hands
6 fresh basil leaves, chopped fine, or ½ teaspoon dried
salt
freshly ground black pepper
3 cups chicken stock
1 pound pasta
2 tablespoons chopped fresh parsley
1 cup freshly grated parmesan cheese

pot in which it cooked. Add the remaining stock, juices and olive bits from the deglazed skillet, and the chicken pieces. Toss well. Sprinkle chopped parsley overall and serve with parmesan cheese.

NOTE
Buy lean chicken with even colored, thin and tight, moist skin. Use clarified butter because you can then cook at a higher temperature without the butter burning. If you prefer to poach the chicken breasts, skin and bone them, then mound the split breasts in a shallow baking dish or saucepan and barely cover with some of the chicken stock. Cover and bake at 425 degrees or simmer on stove for about 15 minutes. The chicken is done when the surface is elastic and white, and juices run clear. Reserve liquid to add to pasta.

WINE
A riesling from Friuli, or other dry white wine

Pasta with Chicken and Sage

1. Combine chicken breasts and lemon juice in a bowl and allow to marinate for 15 minutes. Drain chicken and pat dry.

2. Clarify the butter by putting it in the top of a double boiler over warm water. Turn heat to low and allow butter to melt. When the sediment (a thin milky bubbly substance) has separated from the melted fat (a smooth, somewhat thick, golden liquid), spoon off the sediment and transfer the clear fat to a skillet.

3. In a large skillet, heat the clarified butter to bubbling point and sauté the chicken breasts on both sides until lightly browned. Remove chicken from skillet and slice in ½-inch strips and then again into ½-inch cubes. Place in a bowl.

4. Pour the wine into the skillet and, over high heat, boil liquid until it thickens and pulls away

SERVES 4

INGREDIENTS
4 boned chicken breast halves, skin and fat removed
juice of ½ lemon
4 tablespoons butter
¼ cup dry white wine
6 fresh sage leaves, firmly chopped; or ½ teaspoon crumbled dried sage
salt
freshly ground pepper
1 cup chicken stock, heated
1 pound thin string pasta
½ cup freshly grated parmesan cheese

from pan; this should only take a minute or two. As soon as wine begins to thicken, remove from heat and transfer the liquid to the bowl with the chicken cubes. Add the sage and salt and pepper to taste. Toss lightly and set aside.

5. Cook the pasta until *al dente,* drain, and return it to the pot in which it cooked. Add the chicken and the heated stock. Toss lightly but well, and serve in individual dishes or in a large bowl or platter. Pass the parmesan cheese in a serving bowl.

NOTE
For a dash of elegance and extra freshness, pass a piece of parmesan cheese and a small cheese grater, and allow each diner to grate his or her own sprinkling of parmesan.

WINE
A white sauvignon

Pasta with Truffles and Chicken Parts

This dish can be made with any of the string pastas—spaghettini, vermicelli, fedelini, or fettuccelle.

1. In a skillet, heat 3 tablespoons of the butter, and sauté the gizzards and hearts until they are lightly browned, about 30 minutes. Add chicken livers and more butter if necessary and cook 10 minutes longer. Transfer the chicken pieces to a plate, and keep warm.

2. Add the wine to the skillet and, with a rubber spatula, stir and boil the liquid over high heat until it thickens and pulls away from pan.

3. Add the tomatoes and salt and pepper to taste to the skillet and cook for 5 minutes. Add the chicken pieces to the tomato mixture, and cook an additional 5 minutes over low heat. Add the

SERVES 2 TO 4

INGREDIENTS

4 tablespoons butter
3 chicken gizzards, washed, trimmed, and cut into ¹/₄-inch cubes
3 chicken hearts, washed, trimmed, and cut into ¹/₄-inch cubes
3 chicken livers, washed, picked over, and cut into ¹/₄-inch cubes
¹/₂ cup dry white wine
2 cups fresh tomatoes, peeled, seeded, and chopped into ¹/₂-inch pieces; or 2 cups canned plum tomatoes
salt
freshly ground black pepper
2 truffles, sliced and cut into thinnest strips possible
¹/₂ pound thin pasta
¹/₂ cup freshly grated parmesan cheese (optional)

truffles and cook for 2 minutes. Stir in the remaining 1 tablespoon of butter and blend well.

4. Cook the pasta until *al dente,* drain, and place in a warmed dish. Add the sauce, toss, and serve immediately. Pass the grated parmesan cheese if you wish.

NOTE

If you use canned truffles, drain them and reserve the juice for the sauce.

WINE

A barolo or other robust red wine

Pasta with Meatballs

1. Put the tomatoes through a food mill to purée pulp and remove seeds.

2. In a large skillet or medium saucepan, melt half the butter and cook the onions until soft. Add the garlic, tomato purée, and crumbled bacon. Then add salt and pepper to taste and boil this sauce hard for 3 minutes.

3. Add the marsala and oregano, and cook for another 5 minutes. Set aside.

4. Put all meatball ingredients except the vegetable oil in a bowl, and mix with your hands. Shape the mixture into 12 balls, and in the skillet brown them on all sides in the vegetable oil. Do not overcook; they will cook further in the sauce. Add the meatballs to the tomato sauce and keep warm. (You can brown the meatballs ahead of time and add them to the sauce when you are ready.)

SERVES 4 TO 6

INGREDIENTS

2 cups peeled fresh plum tomatoes or canned Italian plum tomatoes
4 tablespoons butter
2 small onions, chopped fine
1 clove garlic, chopped fine
4 slices bacon, cooked and crumbled
salt and black pepper
½ cup marsala
½ teaspoon dried oregano
½ pound vermicelli
1 cup freshly grated parmesan or romano cheese

MEATBALLS

½ pound ground chuck
2 slices French or Italian bread, moistened with ½ cup milk and squeezed dry
1 tablespoon minced parsley
2 eggs, lightly beaten
¼ cup grated parmesan cheese
salt and ground pepper
3 tablespoons vegetable oil

5. Cook the pasta until *al dente,* drain well, and return to the pot in which it cooked. Add remaining butter and toss well. Add several large spoonfuls of the tomato sauce and toss well again. Transfer pasta to a large serving platter or bowl. Pour sauce and meatballs overall, serve, and pass the cheese.

WINE
A chianti classico

Spaghettini and Veal Birds in a Tomato Sauce

Veal birds are delicious. They come in 2 shapes: a rolled veal cutlet, usually stuffed with parsley, garlic, prosciutto, and parmesan cheese; and a solid piece of meat, the filet of the shank. The second is used in this recipe.

1. In a medium casserole or stainless-steel pot, add the oil and 2 tablespoons of butter and heat to medium high. Add the veal and brown evenly on all sides. When the veal is almost brown (this will take about 10 minutes), add the carrots and celery and sauté for 2 or 3 minutes. Add the shallots and sauté for another few minutes. Add the garlic and sauté an additional 1 minute. Add the wine and cook the mixture until the wine is nearly evaporated. Add the tomatoes and cover. Lower the heat and simmer for 1 hour or until the veal is tender. Add salt and pepper to taste.

SERVES 4

INGREDIENTS
2 tablespoons olive oil
4 tablespoons butter
4 veal birds (filet of the shank)
2 carrots, scraped and cut into ¼-inch cubes
2 stalks celery, scraped and cut into ¼-inch cubes
¼ cup finely chopped shallots
1 large clove garlic, chopped fine
½ cup dry white wine
3 large tomatoes, peeled, seeded, and chopped; or 1½ cups puréed canned Italian plum tomatoes
salt
freshly ground black pepper
½ pound spaghettini
½ cup chicken stock
¼ cup freshly grated locatelli cheese
1 tablespoon finely chopped basil
1 tablespoon finely chopped parsley

2. Cook the spaghettini until *al dente* in rapidly boiling water, drain, and return to the pot in which it cooked. Add the remaining butter and toss well; 2 wooden forks are good utensils to toss with. Add the chicken stock and toss again. Add the cheese and mix well.

3. To assemble, put the pasta in the center of a serving platter and sprinkle the basil and parsley on top. Slice the veal birds lengthwise, and place them around or on top of the spaghettini. Add the tomato sauce *only* on the veal. Serve and pass more cheese.

WINE
A barolo or other robust red wine

Penne with Pork Roast

When we were kids, mom made this dish on Sunday. The pasta sauce is made from cooking the meat, but the roast is eaten as the second course.

1. Chop the garlic, parsley, and salt pork together, combining them to almost paste form. Cut 3 or 4 incisions in the pork loin and fill them with the paste.

2. In a casserole over medium heat, heat 2 tablespoons of the butter and 1 tablespoon of the oil. Add the pork loin, sprinkle with salt and pepper, and brown it evenly on all sides. Remove the meat, then pour off the fat from the casserole.

3. Preheat the oven to 300 degrees. Heat the remaining 2 tablespoons of oil in the casserole. Add the onions, carrot, and celery and sauté 5 minutes. Add the oregano, basil, red pepper flakes, wine, tomato purée, and tomatoes and

SERVES 6

INGREDIENTS
1 large clove garlic
2 tablespoons chopped flat parsley
¼ cup cubed salt pork
1 2-pound piece lean pork loin
5 tablespoons butter
3 tablespoons olive oil
salt
freshly ground black pepper
3 medium yellow onions, finely chopped
1 carrot, scraped and finely chopped
1 stalk celery, scraped and finely chopped
½ teaspoon dried oregano
½ teaspoon dried basil
pinch of red pepper flakes
1 cup red wine
½ cup tomato purée
1 can (1 pound, 12 ounces) Italian plum tomatoes, put through a food mill
1 pound penne
Parmesan cheese

simmer for 10 minutes, stirring occasionally. Return the pork loin to the casserole, cover, and cook in oven for 2½ hours or until the meat is tender. Remove the fat that collects on the top. Adjust the seasoning.

4. Cook the penne until *al dente,* drain well, and return to the pot in which it cooked. Add the remaining butter and toss well. Serve as the pasta course with the sauce spooned on top and pass the cheese at the table. Serve the pork loin after the pasta course by slicing in ½-inch slices (or thicker, if preferred). This is good accompanied by a crisp salad.

WINE
A pinot nero or other full-bodied red wine

Egg and Spinach Pastas with Ham, Mushrooms, and Cream

This is the exquisite paglia e fieno, *which means "straw and hay." It combines egg and spinach pasta in one of the prettiest dishes to present.*

1. Wipe the mushrooms clean and trim stems. Cut into ¼-inch cubes and set aside.

2. In a large skillet, melt 4 tablespoons of the butter and sauté the shallots over medium heat until they have turned pale gold. Turn up the heat and add the mushrooms. Cook the mushrooms until they absorb the butter, then lower the heat. Add 1 teaspoon salt and mill in some pepper, tossing the mushrooms in the skillet with a wooden spoon or by shaking the pan. The mushrooms will render juice quickly; at this point, turn the heat up high again and cook the mushrooms for 3 minutes. Stir frequently! Reduce the heat, add the ham, and cook for only 1 minute. Add half the heavy cream all at once and cook just long enough for the cream to thicken slightly. Taste and add salt and pepper to taste. Remove from the heat.

3. In a large saucepan, melt the remaining 4 tablespoons of butter and add the remaining cream. Turn on the heat low. When the butter is melted and amalgamated with cream, remove from heat.

4. Cook the 2 pastas in separate pots, since spinach pasta cooks faster than egg pasta. Drain well and transfer both to the pan with the butter and cream. Drain the egg noodles and transfer them to the same pan. Turn the heat to low and toss the noodles, coating them with the cream mixture. Add the peas, then add half the mushroom sauce, mixing it well with the pasta. Add ½ cup of cheese and quickly mix it with the pasta. Remove from heat and transfer to a bowl Pour in rest of sauce and serve with additional cheese.

SERVES 6 TO 8

INGREDIENTS
¾ pound fresh mushrooms
¼ pound butter
¼ cup finely chopped shallots
6 ounces unsmoked boiled ham, cut into julienne strips, or 4 ounces prosciutto or other salami
1 cup heavy cream
salt
freshly ground pepper
½ cup fresh or frozen peas, cooked
¾ pound fresh fettuccine
½ pound spinach fettuccine
½ to 1 cup freshly grated parmesan cheese

WINE
A chianti from the Colline Senesi, or another medium-bodied red wine

Penne with Sausage and Mushrooms

Luganega sausage is found in all Italian meat markets and many American ones as well. It is a long coil of sausage, not tied into links. Cut the sausage into 1- or 2-inch lengths when it is extremely cold, almost half frozen.

1. Sauté the sausage in butter and olive oil until the meat is brown, about 15 minutes. Add the mushrooms and cook over low heat for 10 minutes. Stir in the garlic and peas, and salt and pepper to taste.

SERVES 4

INGREDIENTS

1 pound luganega sausage
3 tablespoons butter
3 tablespoons olive oil
½ pound fresh mushrooms, sliced thin
1 clove garlic, chopped fine
½ cup fresh or frozen green peas, cooked
salt
freshly ground black pepper
1 pound penne
1 cup freshly grated parmesan cheese

2. Cook the penne until *al dente*. Drain and return to the pot in which it cooked. Add half the cheese and half the sauce. Toss well, then transfer to a warmed bowl. Add the remaining sauce and serve. Pass remaining cheese.

WINE

A good red wine, such as pinot nero

Pasta with Coppa and Eggs

This dish is known as alla carbonara. It is a Roman dish that's a welcome change from the customary pasta with tomato sauce. It can be made with any shaped pasta.

1. In a skillet, heat the butter and sauté the coppa pieces for 2 minutes, stirring frequently. Remove from the heat and set aside.

2. Cook the pasta until *al dente,* then drain and put it in a heated dish. Keep warm.

3. Return the skillet with the coppa to the heat. Add the beaten eggs to the coppa and stir as you would for scrambled eggs. Then pour the egg mixture onto the pasta at the precise moment when the eggs are beginning to thicken,

SERVES 4 TO 6

INGREDIENTS
2 tablespoons butter
4 ounces coppa, cut into
  2-inch matchsticks
1 pound pasta
2 eggs, lightly beaten
1 cup freshly grated parmesan
  cheese

so that they present a slightly granulated appearance without being as thick as scrambled eggs. Stir the pasta mixture with a wooden spoon so that the egg and bacon mixture is evenly distributed, add half the parmesan cheese, and serve immediately with remaining parmesan separately.

WINE
A barbera del monferrato, or other robust red wine

Spaghetti Frittata with Pancetta and Peas

Utterly charming and delicious, this can be prepared ahead and transported to a picnic or enjoyed later. Serve with a salad to complete the meal.

1. In a medium pot, bring 5 or 6 cups of water to a boil. Add 1 teaspoon of salt and cook the spaghetti pieces for 5 minutes, until *al dente.* Drain and set aside for a few minutes.

2. In a medium bowl, combine the eggs, cooked spaghetti, mozzarella, and salt and pepper to taste. Mix well and set aside. In another small bowl, add the pancetta, peas, and parmesan cheese. Mix gently until well combined.

3. In a 9- or 10-inch skillet (be sure to use a pan that does not stick), heat the oil over medium-high heat until hot (not smoking). Add the garlic and sauté for 1 minute.

SERVES 4 TO 6

INGREDIENTS

1 cup spaghetti, broken into 2-inch pieces and cooked al dente
4 eggs, lightly beaten
1 cup freshly grated mozzarella cheese
salt
freshly ground black pepper
6 very thin slices pancetta, cut into small pieces and cooked until crisp
1 cup fresh or frozen peas, lightly cooked
1/3 cup freshly grated parmesan cheese
3 tablespoons olive oil
2 small cloves garlic, chopped fine

4. Pour half the egg-and-spaghetti mixture into the skillet and top with the pancetta, peas, and cheese. Cover with the remaining egg-and-spaghetti mixture. Turn the heat to medium high and cook, pressing the frittata down lightly. Cook for 8 minutes or until underside is a golden brown.

5. Invert the frittata onto a plate and slide it back into the pan. (You may need to add a little more oil to the pan for this step.) Cook the underside for 5 minutes or less, or until golden brown.

6. Serve warm, or allow to cool for later. It is especially good if served cool on a hot day with sliced fresh tomatoes on the side, dotted with olive oil and fresh basil.

WINE
A carema or other full-bodied red wine

Fedelini with White Clam Sauce

Fedelini, which means "the faithful," is one of the thinnest of the rope or string pasta; it's thinner than vermicelli. When you make your pasta, roll it out as thin as possible, then roll it lightly in folds about 4 inches wide, starting with the edge closest to you. When the circle of pasta is so folded, cut into the thinnest slices possible.

1. Scrub the clams thoroughly with a stiff wire brush, rinsing them several times. Soak in cool fresh water for 30 minutes or longer to remove any sand in the clams. Remove the clams by hand from the bowl or pan in which you soaked them (sand will have sunk to the bottom), then place the clams in a heavy covered saucepan, along with half the garlic and about 4 tablespoons of olive oil. Cover, and steam over medium heat until the clams open, about 10 to 15 minutes. Do not overcook. Discard any clams that have not opened. When you separate the clams from their shells,

SERVES 4

INGREDIENTS

5 dozen littleneck clams, or 3 cans (7½ ounces each) minced clams
2 large cloves garlic, chopped fine
½ cup olive oil
4 tablespoons butter
1 carrot, scraped and chopped very fine
½ cup finely chopped scallions or onions
1 cup clam juice
1 cup dry white wine
pinch of red pepper flakes
salt
8 sprigs parsley, stems removed and leaves chopped fine
1 pound fedelini

retain all the juice you can for the sauce. Cut clams in half or thirds. Set clams and juice aside.

2. In a large skillet, heat the remaining oil and the butter. Add the carrot pieces, and sauté for about 5 minutes. Add the scallions and remaining garlic, and cook for several minutes until they begin to brown lightly. Add all the juice from the fresh clams (or the juice from the canned clams), the additional 1 cup of clam juice, and the white wine. Put in the red pepper flakes, then boil for 10 or 15 minutes to allow most of the wine to cook off. Add salt to taste, and adjust the red pepper seasoning. (Don't make it too hot.)

3. Cook the pasta until *al dente,* drain, and return to the pot. Add the clams and parsley, then the sauce. Toss and serve.

WINE
A full, fruity white wine, such as albano secco

Mussels with Green Pasta

This is a glorious dish, unmistakenly tasty.

1. Wash the mussels with a stiff brush, remove the beards, and place in large bowl. Cover with water and let stand for 3 to 4 hours, changing the water several times to get rid of the sand. Drain, and put mussels in a large covered saucepan. Add the garlic and the wine. Cover the pan, and steam the mussels over low heat until the shells open. Discard any unopened ones. Remove the mussels from their shells, being careful to capture all the juice for the sauce. Discard the shells.

2. Cook the pasta until it is *al dente*. Drain, and return it to the saucepan in which it cooked. Add the butter, olive oil, lemon juice, and reserved juice from the steamed mussels. Add half the mussels and half the fresh tomatoes and toss well.

SERVES 4 TO 6

INGREDIENTS
48 to 54 fresh mussels
1 clove garlic, halved
1 cup dry white wine
1 pound green pasta
2 tablespoons butter
⅓ cup olive oil
¼ cup fresh lemon juice
3 firm medium tomatoes, peeled, seeded, and chopped into ½-inch pieces (do not use canned tomatoes)

3. Empty the mixture of pasta and sauce into a large bowl or platter, or divide for individual servings. Arrange the remaining mussels and tomato pieces on top of the pasta. The cool, uncooked tomato pieces contribute to a wonderful combination of textures and tastes.

WINE
A full and fruity white wine such as greco di Tufo from near Naples or a vernaccia di San Gimignano from Tuscany

Pasta with Bay Scallops

1. Marinate the bay scallops in the lemon juice for 30 minutes.

2. Prepare the sauce first. In a skillet, heat the oil and butter and sauté the shallots until they begin to turn color. Add the wine, tomatoes, clam juice, fennel, salt, and pepper. Bring to a boil, lower the heat, and allow to simmer for 10 minutes.

3. Drain and sauté the scallops in 2 tablespoons butter over high heat for 3 minutes. Add to the sauce for the last minute of cooking.

SERVES 4 TO 6

INGREDIENTS
1 pound fresh bay scallops
juice of ½ lemon
4 tablespoons butter
1 pound capellini
½ cup chopped fresh parsley (not dried)
1 tablespoon finely chopped lemon zest

SAUCE
4 tablespoons olive oil
4 tablespoons butter
8 shallots, sliced fine
½ cup white wine
1 cup puréed canned Italian plum tomatoes
12 ounces clam juice
½ teaspoon fennel seed
freshly ground black pepper
salt

4. Cook the pasta until *al dente,* and return it to the pot in which it cooked. Add the remaining butter and toss lightly. Add the sauce with the scallops, the parsley, and the lemon zest and serve immediately.

WINE
A full and fruity white wine such as malvasia del Collio or pinot bianco

Tagliolini with Crabmeat

1. In a saucepan, heat the butter and oil, and sauté the onions, celery, and garlic until soft. Add the parsley, salt, pepper, paprika, and fish broth and cook over low heat for 10 minutes. Stir in the crabmeat and simmer for 5 minutes. Adjust seasoning.

SERVES 4 TO 6

INGREDIENTS

3 tablespoons butter
3 tablespoons olive oil
3 small white onions, chopped
3 inner celery ribs, scraped and chopped
2 cloves garlic, chopped fine
3 tablespoons chopped fresh flat parsley
1 teaspoon salt
½ teaspoon black pepper
1½ teaspoons paprika
1 cup fish broth or clam juice
1 pound fresh or canned crabmeat, shell and cartilage removed, flaked
1 pound tagliolini

2. Cook the pasta until *al dente,* drain, and toss with half the sauce. Spoon the remaining sauce on top of the individual servings, or in a large bowl. Serve.

WINE
A full and fruity white wine such as pinot blanco

Lobster and White Wine in a Fresh Tomato Sauce

Tomato sauce accented with herbs and lightly sautéed lobster make an exciting, flavorful pasta dish.

1. Heat the butter in a large, heavy enameled skillet or a large saucepan. Add the lobster and cook quickly over high heat for about 1 minute, stirring frequently. Using a slotted spoon, transfer the lobster pieces to a small bowl, and set aside.

2. In the same pan, heat the olive oil. Add the garlic and shallots, and cook until they turn golden (about 5 minutes), being careful not to let them brown. Pour in the wine, and cook for another 5 minutes so that the liquor can cook away.

3. Remove pan from the heat, and add the tomato paste, basil, oregano, and lemon zest. Mix

SERVES 4

INGREDIENTS
4 tablespoons butter
2 cups cooked lobster meat, cut into ½-inch pieces
4 tablespoons olive oil
2 cloves garlic, chopped fine
¼ cup finely chopped shallots
½ cup dry white wine
1 tablespoon tomato paste
2 tablespoons finely chopped fresh basil
1 teaspoon dried oregano
1 teaspoon finely chopped zest of lemon peel
6 large fresh tomatoes, peeled, seeded, and cut into ½-inch cubes; or 4 cups canned Italian plum tomatoes with a little liquid
salt
freshly ground black pepper
1 pound thin pasta
2 tablespoons finely chopped shallots
1 tablespoon finely chopped fresh parsley

well, then add the fresh or canned tomatoes. Return pan to the heat and bring tomato sauce to a boil, then lower heat and simmer for about 15 minutes.

4. Remove the pan from the heat and add the lobster meat and salt and pepper to taste. Stir well and keep sauce warm while you are cooking the pasta.

5. Cook the pasta until *al dente,* drain, and return to pot in which it cooked. Add sauce to pasta, and toss. Combine the chopped shallots with the parsley and sprinkle over the pasta.

WINE
A santa maddalena from the Tyrol, or other dry white wine

On the following pages: Duck Lasagne with Porcini and Truffles (recipe on page 143); Tubetti and Gorgonzola Salad (recipe on page 171).

Squid and Shrimp with Spaghettini

Squid can be twice as delicious as lobster and only half the trouble.

1. Lay the squid on a flat surface in front of you, and stretch it lengthwise from left to right, tentacles to your right. With a sharp knife, cut just below the eyes; this will free the tentacles. There are 10 tentacles, and in the center of them is the mouth; pull or cut it off and discard it. Pull off whatever skin you can from the tentacles, but don't be concerned if you don't get much off. (We always use the tentacles; chopped up in a stuffing is one way.) Squeeze the body, and pull the head out; the viscera will come out of the body easily; discard all this. Now pull out the transparent center bone (the chitinous pen or quill). What remains of the squid is a sack. Wash this well and peel off the outer skin, which is purply gray and membranelike; it pulls off easily. Wash the squid well and

SERVES 4 TO 6

INGREDIENTS
12 fresh baby squid (calamari)
24 medium shrimp
juice of 1 lemon
10 tablespoons butter
2 tablespoons olive oil
1 teaspoon salt
freshly ground black pepper
1 cup fish stock or clam juice
1 pound spaghettini

WINE
A white corvo or other dry, light wine

slice it crosswise to make thin circles, or cut it lengthwise.

2. Peel the shrimp and devein. Wash carefully. Dry and combine with lemon juice. Set aside.

3. In a large skillet, heat 8 tablespoons of butter and the oil until the butter is melted and bubbly. Add the squid pieces and sauté for 15 minutes or until tender.

4. Five minutes before the squid are done, add the shrimp and sauté until they turn pink and are done. Do not overcook the shrimp. Add the salt.

5. Cook the pasta until *al dente,* drain well, and return to the pot in which it cooked. Toss the pasta with the remaining 2 tablespoons of butter and add ground pepper to taste. Add the fish stock or clam juice and half the squid-shrimp mixture. Toss well and transfer to a large platter or individual plates. Add the remaining squid and shrimp and serve.

Thin Spaghetti with a Rich Seafood Sauce

1. Bring the stock and the vermouth to a boil. Add the squid pieces, lower the heat, and simmer for 25 minutes.

2. Add the lobster and clams and cook for 2 minutes longer, then add the fish. Cook an additional 2 minutes. The fish pieces will cook very quickly; you'll know they are done when they turn white. Do not overcook.

3. Add the butter and stir gently. Try not to break the filet pieces, although they invariably will flake apart a little; the point is not to end up with fish looking like mashed potatoes. Remove from heat and set aside.

4. Cook the thin spaghetti until *al dente,* drain, and transfer to a large, deep platter or bowl. Pour the fish and sauce overall, garnish with parsley and scallion pieces, and serve immediately.

SERVES 6

INGREDIENTS

4 cups lean rich fish stock or clam juice
½ cup dry vermouth
¼ pound squid pieces
1 pound lobster claws, chopped
½ pound finely chopped clams, preferably fresh, but canned will do
1 pound filets of sole or other whitefish, cut into large chunks
2 tablespoons butter
salt
freshly ground black pepper
1 pound thin spaghetti
2 tablespoons chopped fresh parsley
1 tablespoon finely chopped scallions

NOTE

If you don't have time to clean fresh squid (although fresh cleaned squid is often available at a fish store), you might substitute canned or frozen squid. If frozen, allow to come to room temperature and chop into 1-inch squares or slice very thin.

WINE

A tocai from Friuli or other dry, medium-bodied white wine

Linguini with Anchovy and Caper Sauce

1. Soak the anchovy filets in cool water for 30 minutes. Drain, pat dry, and chop finely. Set aside.

2. In a skillet, heat the oil and sauté the garlic until it turns to a light brown. Remove the garlic with a slotted spoon and discard.

3. To the skillet, add the capers, olives, parsley, water, and pepper and cook for 5 minutes. Remove from the heat.

4. Add the anchovies to the skillet and, with a wooden spoon, stir until the anchovies dissolve into the olive oil sauce.

SERVES 4

INGREDIENTS
8 flat anchovy filets
½ cup olive oil
2 cloves garlic, peeled and cut in half
½ cup capers, rinsed
1 cup pitted black olives
¼ cup finely chopped flat parsley
3 tablespoons water
freshly ground black pepper
1 pound linguini

5. Cook the linguini until *al dente,* drain, and transfer to a warm bowl. Pour the sauce over-all, toss lightly, and serve immediately.

WINE
A full-bodied red wine such as chianti or gattinara

Spaghettini with Italian Tuna

This is a very simple, classical dish, easy to prepare and with a great deal of taste. The sauce can be made ahead and kept in the refrigerator for several days. In fact, the tuna and other ingredients combine so well that one or two days later the sauce is significantly more flavorful.

1. In a large skillet, heat the olive oil and sauté the garlic over moderate heat until it has just begun to turn color. Add the parsley and cook for 1 minute more.

2. Add the tomatoes with their juice, lower the heat, stir frequently, and cook uncovered for about 30 minutes or until the tomatoes separate from the oil.

3. With a fork, separate the tuna into tiny pieces. Add to the tomato mixture after it has cooked for 30 minutes and the tomatoes have separated from the oil. Add salt to taste, but remember that the tuna is salty to begin

SERVES 4 TO 6

INGREDIENTS

¼ cup olive oil
3 cloves garlic, chopped fine
¼ cup finely chopped parsley
1½ cups seeded and chopped canned Italian plum tomatoes, with some liquid
1 can (10 ounces) Italian tuna packed in oil, drained
salt to taste
freshly ground black pepper
1 pound spaghettini
4 tablespoons butter

with. Grate your freshly ground pepper directly into the skillet and cook this mixture uncovered at a very bare simmer for 5 minutes.

4. Cook the spaghettini until *al dente,* drain it, and be sure to shake the colander so that as much liquid is removed as possible. Return the pasta to the pan in which it cooked. Add 4 tablespoons of butter and, with 1 or 2 wooden forks, toss lightly until all strands of the pasta are coated with the butter. Mix two-thirds of the sauce into the pasta, toss lightly again, and distribute among individual plates or put into a large serving bowl or platter. Pour the remaining sauce over the pasta and serve immediately.

WINE
A sangiovese di romagna or other dry, medium-bodied red wine

Spaghetti with Anchovies, Tuna, and Peas

Another delicious tuna sauce, served hot.

1. In a large skillet, heat 3 tablespoons of the butter and the olive oil. When bubbling, sauté the onions for 5 minutes; do not allow them to brown. Add the anchovies (and the oil from the container) to the onions and, with a wooden spoon or fork, mash the anchovies until they amalgamate into the sauce.

2. Boil the fresh peas in salted water until tender; do not overcook. If using frozen peas, drop them in boiling, salted water until thawed thoroughly. Fresh or frozen, drain well and set aside for adding to pasta after it is cooked.

SERVES 4

INGREDIENTS

5 tablespoons butter
3 tablespoons olive oil
2 medium white onions, chopped fine
1 can (2 ounces) flat anchovy filets packed in olive oil
1 pound fresh green peas, shelled; or 1 package (10 ounces) frozen peas, thawed
1 can (7 ounces) Italian tuna packed in oil, drained
1 cup heavy cream
freshly ground black pepper
1 pound spaghetti

3. Break up the tuna into flakes and add it to the onion/anchovy mixture. Stir well and heat through. Add the cream and bring just to a boil. Add plenty of pepper. Keep the sauce warm.

4. Cook the spaghetti until *al dente* and return it to the pan in which it cooked. Add the remaining butter, toss lightly; add the peas and sauce. Toss again, and serve.

WINE

A rossese di dolceacqua or other dry red wine

Codfish with Tiny Pasta Shells

Salted codfish seems to be the characteristic aroma of every Italian market, wherever it may be. Baccala (dried codfish) is a food we grew up with; children had to eat it on Christmas Eve, or there would be an empty sock at the mantle the next morning. Even these days, Christmas Eve doesn't seem quite complete to us without baccala.

1. In a large pan or bowl, soak the codfish in water to cover for at least 24 hours. Change the water frequently. Drain the codfish and put it in a covered ovenproof pan or dish. Add enough milk so that the fish is just barely covered. Put the garlic clove in with the fish and milk, cover the pan or dish, and bake in a preheated 350-degree oven for 25 to 30 minutes, or until the fish is tender.

SERVES 4 TO 6

INGREDIENTS

1 piece salted dry codfish, about ¾ to 1 pound
2 cups milk
1 small clove garlic
4 tablespoons olive oil
2 tablespoons butter, softened
freshly ground black pepper
1 cup heavy cream
1 pound conchigliette or equivalent tiny pasta shells

2. Drain the fish, discard the milk, but reserve the garlic clove. Remove the bones and skin from the cod, and discard. Flake the fish. (It's easy to do this with your hands.) Purée the cod and garlic clove in a food processor, adding the oil a little at a time, then the butter, and then the pepper. Add the heavy cream until you've achieved a smooth, creamy mixture. Do not overbeat.

3. Cook the conchigliette until *al dente,* and return to the pan in which it cooked. Combine the fish sauce with the conchigliette, toss well, and serve on a large platter, in a large bowl, in individual bowls, or on individual plates. Sprinkle some freshly ground pepper overall.

WINE
A full-bodied white wine such as pinot blanco

Rotelle with Red Snapper Sauce

Fresh red snapper filets are the basis for this refreshing pasta sauce, which is spooned over rotelle (little wheels).

1. In a heavy saucepan, heat the olive oil and add the red pepper, onion, garlic, and anchovies. Cook for 5 minutes, stirring frequently; use a wooden spoon or rubber spatula to dissolve the anchovies.

2. Add the tomatoes, sprinkle liberally with freshly ground pepper (this sauce should have a spark or two), and cook for an additional 10 minutes. Add the red snapper and lemon juice, and cook until the fish is tender and flaky. This will not take long (only a couple of minutes), so keep your eye on it. Test a piece of fish with a fork for doneness—if the fish breaks apart, or flakes, it is done.

SERVES 4

INGREDIENTS

3 tablespoons olive oil
1 large red bell pepper, cored, seeded, and cut into ½-inch cubes
1 medium onion, sliced fine
1 clove garlic, chopped fine
6 anchovy filets
3 cups peeled, seeded and chopped fresh or canned plum tomatoes
freshly ground black pepper
1 pound red snapper filets, washed, dried, and cut into 1- to 1½-inch squares
1 teaspoon lemon juice
1 pound rotelle
2 tablespoons butter
6 sprigs fresh flat leaf parsley, stems removed, and leaves chopped fine

3. While the sauce is cooking, cook the rotelle until *al dente*. Drain the pasta, and return it to the pot in which it cooked. Add the butter, and toss well. Put the pasta on a large serving platter or on individual plates, add the sauce, and serve. Garnish with parsley.

WINE
A pinot blanco or other dry, light white wine

Straw and Hay Pasta with Salmon

1. Cut the salmon lengthwise into 1½-inch widths. Cut each piece on the bias into 1½-inch lengths. Set aside.

2. In a skillet, heat half the butter and add the shallots and hot red pepper. Cook about 30 seconds, stirring all the time. Then add the salmon pieces and cook about 1 minute, tossing them gently. Add the wine and cook another 1 minute longer. Add salt and pepper to taste.

3. Add the cream and, when it returns to a boil, cook over high heat about 3 or 4 minutes. Add the nutmeg. Turn off the heat and set the skillet aside.

4. Green pasta will cook faster than the other pasta, so they will have to be boiled in separate pans. Bring about 4 quarts of water to a boil in each pan and add salt and oil. Add the green noodles first and bring to a boil, stir-

SERVES 4 TO 6

INGREDIENTS

1½ pounds skinless, boneless salmon filets
8 tablespoons butter
⅓ cup finely chopped shallots
1 small dried hot red pepper, seeded and chopped
¼ cup dry white wine
salt
freshly ground pepper
1 cup heavy cream
½ pound egg pasta, or dried imported, yellow noodle "nests"
½ pound green pasta, or dried imported, green noodle "nests"
⅓ teaspoon freshly grated nutmeg
¼ cup finely chopped basil
¼ cup finely chopped chives

ring; then bring another large pot of water to a boil and cook the other pasta. Cook both until *al dente,* drain well, and return both pastas to 1 pot.

5. Add the remaining butter and toss. Pour the pasta onto a large serving platter. Pour the salmon and sauce over the pasta. Toss gently. Sprinkle with the basil and chives and serve immediately.

NOTE
Noodle "nests" are available at most stores that carry pasta; most ¬upermarkets carry them and surely do the specialty pasta and Italian food shops.

WINE
A lago di caldaro or other dry, light-bodied red wine

BAKED AND MOLDED PASTAS

*O*ut of the cornucopia of the Italian kitchen comes pasta that is exuberant. Pasta preparations, profuse with precious ingredients, are entirely baroque in their never-ending exploration of every tasty, happy, and comforting combination of flavor and texture. The combinations often offer a mystique, especially when pasta is used as a shield, a foil, a crust, a covering or whatever—a spoon or knife inserted into the dish or mold will bring forth a total surprise. This chapter of baked and molded preparations is living proof of the quality of Italian cooking. Herein is pasta, concealed or out in the open, in a multitude of riches.

Pasta Primavera Mold

One of the most spectacular pasta preparations in this book, great for a buffet or dinner party appetizer.

1. Clean each vegetable by paring, washing, stringing, and slicing where necessary. Cook the asparagus, broccoli, and peas separately in boiling salted water until *al dente.* Do not overcook.

2. In a saucepan, heat chicken stock, cream, garlic, mushrooms, and pepper flakes. As soon as this comes to a boil, remove it from the heat.

3. In a large bowl, combine eggs, cheese, and parsley and mix well. Add the cream mixture and stir well.

4. Heat ½ tablespoon butter in a small skillet and sauté the snow peas for 1 minute. Remove from heat and set aside. Preheat oven to 350 degrees.

INGREDIENTS

32 asparagus spears
2 cups fresh broccoli florets
8 fresh snow peas, cut into
  ½-inch pieces on bias
  (½ cup)
½ pound fresh green peas,
  shelled, or ½ package
  (10 ounces) frozen
½ cup rich chicken broth,
  cooked down to ¼ cup
½ cup heavy cream
3 cloves garlic, finely chopped
½ ounce finely chopped dried
  mushrooms
pinch of red pepper flakes
6 eggs
¾ cup freshly grated
  parmesan cheese
2 tablespoons chopped fresh
  parsley
2½ tablespoons butter
½ pound Broccoli Pasta
  (page 62) or egg pasta
  fettuccine
½ cup toasted pinenuts

5. Cook the pasta just below *al dente* point. (It will cook more in the oven.) Drain it and return it to the pan in which it cooked. Add 2 tablespoons butter and toss. Add the cream and egg mixture to the pasta combining it all thoroughly.

6. Liberally butter a mold, 3½ inches deep and 8¼ inches wide at top. (A French soufflé dish is excellent.) Cut out a circle of wax paper to fit the bottom of the baking dish. Butter the top side of the paper. Arrange the broccoli florets on the bottom of the mold, flower sides down; there are enough flowers to cover the bottom of the baking dish. Arrange the asparagus stalks, after cutting to the size of the depth of the mold, standing up with the flower side of the asparagus pointed to the bottom of the mold.

7. Transfer the pasta mixture to the mold. Set the mold in a large vessel filled with hot water (to serve as a *bain marie*), and set both in oven for 50 minutes. Remove baking dish from the oven and from the *bain marie*. Return baking dish to oven and cook for 30 minutes longer. Remove from oven. The mold *must* rest for 15 minutes or longer to turn out properly. Take a large serving plate, put it over the mold, reverse it, and allow it to sit. Before turning it over, run a thin sharp knife around the outer edge of the mold to ease the turning out procedure. There should be *no* juices visible in the mold; the mold should be set, as in custard. Lift off the paper.

8. When it is turned out, sprinkle the toasted pinenuts overall. Serve by slicing through as you would cut a cake. Serve with tomato sauce given on page 34, or without a sauce if you serve it as a vegetable or buffet dish. The tomato sauce should be spooned onto each serving plate, on the side of the pasta serving, not directly over it.

WINE
A chianti classico or other dry, medium-bodied red wine

Swiss Chard and Pasta Timbales

These timbales not only are delicious tasting, but they are lovely to look at. They make an excellent companion to meat dishes or elegant first course.

1. Put the chard in a blender with 1 tablespoon of cream and purée. Transfer to a large bowl and add the fontina and parmesan cheeses, eggs, and remaining cream. Combine well. Preheat the oven to 375 degrees.

2. In a medium pan, cook the pasta in boiling, salted water for 2 minutes. Drain and return it to the pan in which it cooked, add 2 tablespoons of the butter and toss well. Add the pasta to the chard mixture. Add salt and pepper to taste.

3. Have ready 6 custard cups 3½ inches by 2 inches. Butter each cup, then fill the cups to the top with the chard mixture. Place cups in a roasting pan; put 3 cups of hot water in the roasting pan. Cover the top with wax paper and

SERVES 6

INGREDIENTS

½ pound fresh swiss chard, cooked and drained then chopped very fine (about 1 cup)
1 cup half and half
1 cup grated fontina cheese
¼ cup freshly grated parmesan cheese
2 eggs, lightly beaten
¼ pound tagliolini, cut in 3-inch pieces
3 tablespoons butter
salt
freshly ground black pepper
1 small carrot, cut into julienne pieces, ¼ by 2 inches

set in the oven; bake for 20 or 25 minutes. Remove from the oven and carefully lift out the cups. Let sit a few minutes. Unmold the timbales onto a serving platter. Set aside for a few minutes.

4. In a small skillet, melt the remaining tablespoon of butter on medium high heat and add the carrots along with 2 or 3 tablespoons of water. Cover with a piece of wax paper and cook for a few minutes. Remove and drain.

5. Add 3 or 4 pieces of carrots decoratively on top, or leaning against the sides of each timbale. Serve immediately.

NOTE
The carrots can be prepared 2 or 3 hours before serving the timbales. Cover with piece of wax paper or foil to reduce drying out.

WINE
A valpolicella or other dry, medium-bodied red wine

Baked Fettuccine

This is fun to prepare, wonderful to look at, and delicious to eat. It can be served as a pasta side dish with meats or as a luncheon dish with fresh salad greens dressed with oil and vinegar.

SERVES 6 TO 8

INGREDIENTS

1 pound fettuccine
7 tablespoons butter
¼ cup grated parmesan cheese
1 cup heavy cream
1 pound fontina cheese, cut into small pieces
freshly ground black pepper
½ cup fine bread crumbs
1 egg

1. Cook the fettuccine in boiling, salted water until *al dente,* and drain them. Put them back in the pan in which they were cooked, and add 3 tablespoons of butter, parmesan cheese, heavy cream, fontina cheese, and freshly ground pepper.

2. Preheat the oven to 350 degrees. Butter well an oval ovenproof casserole (approximately 9 by 14 by 2 inches, preferably clear glass). Add ¼ cup bread crumbs, and tilt the baking dish back and forth to cover the entire surface of the dish with crumbs. Empty the extra crumbs onto a sheet of wax paper. Beat the egg well in a small bowl, and pour it into the crumbled baking dish. Tilt the dish again to cover all the crumbs with the egg. Add the remaining ¼ cup bread crumbs, and tilt again to cover the surface completely. Turn out and discard the excess crumbs.

3. With a rubber spatula, transfer all the pasta, scraping the sides and bottom of the pan, into the double-crusted baking dish. Place this in oven, and bake for 15 minutes, or until heated through. (If the baking dish is clear glass, you'll be able to see the crust turn a golden brown, and you will know it's ready.) Remove from the oven, and allow to sit for 10 to 15 minutes.

4. Turn the timballo out onto a large oval platter and garnish with a sprig of fresh parsley. This is a very handsome and tasty dish.

WINE
A white sauvignon or other dry white wine

Pasta Wheels and Prosciutto with Asparagus Spears

1. In a small skillet, melt 1 tablespoon of butter and sauté the scallions for 1 or 2 minutes. Add garlic and sauté for 2 minutes or until lightly brown. Transfer scallions and garlic to a large bowl.

2. In same skillet, add remaining tablespoon of butter and sauté mushrooms for 2 minutes. Add to scallions and garlic and set aside.

3. Preheat the oven to 350 degrees. In a medium pot, boil 6 cups of water. Cook the pasta wheels for 5 minutes; *no longer.* Drain the pasta and return it to the pot in which it cooked. Add the milk and stir briefly. Add the fontina, the mushroom mixture, and the diced prosciutto. Season with salt and pepper.

4. In a small bowl, beat the eggs with a hand electric beater or with an egg beater and whip until light and fluffy. Add the eggs to the pasta mixture and mix well. Preheat the oven to 350 degrees.

SERVES 6

INGREDIENTS

2 tablespoons butter
½ cup finely chopped scallions, including some light green parts
1 clove garlic, chopped fine
1 cup sliced fresh mushrooms
2 cups pasta wheels (rotelle)
1½ cups milk
1 cup thinly sliced fontina cheese
½ pound finely sliced prosciutto; half reserved for asparagus, half diced finely
1 teaspoon salt
freshly ground black pepper
4 eggs, at room temperature
15 asparagus spears

NOTE

This pasta mold is also delicious served cold. Another time fill it with buttered broccoli florets.

5. Butter a 9 by 5-inch ring mold and spoon the pasta-and-egg mixture into the mold. Place the ring mold in a large roasting pan and add about 3 inches of water to the pan, about half way up the mold.

6. Bake about 45 minutes or until a knife inserted into the center comes out clean. Remove the mold from the oven and let stand for approximately 10 minutes before inverting onto a serving plate.

7. While the mold rests, steam the asparagus spears until *al dente,* about 3 or 4 minutes. Let cool slightly and then wrap each asparagus spear with a thin slice of prosciutto. Invert the pasta mold and arrange the asparagus spears in the center of the mold.

WINE

A chianti from the Colline Senesi or other robust red wine

Pasta Rustica

1. In a skillet, heat the oil and sauté the sausage pieces until lightly brown, about 5 minutes. Combine the sausage with all other ingredients except the lasagne strips, and set aside.

2. Cook the lasagne strips (4 at a time) in boiling, salted water until just below the *al dente* point. Drain and lay on kitchen cotton towel. Pat dry with toweling.

3. Preheat the oven to 350 degrees. Liberally butter a 9 by 2 or 3-inch round baking dish and arrange 4 lasagne strips by putting the end of 1 strip in the center of the baking dish and running it to the edge, up the side and with an overhang. Repeat this procedure, slightly overlapping each pasta strip until the baking dish is covered with lasagne.

4. Fill the dish with half the filling and overlap the lasagne strips to cover the filling. Add the other half of the filling and cover with

SERVES 8 TO 12

INGREDIENTS

2 tablespoons olive oil
½ pound Italian sweet sausage, sliced thin
½ pound boiled ham, in ½-inch dice
1 cup freshly grated mozzarella cheese
½ cup freshly grated parmesan cheese
6 eggs, lightly beaten
¼ pound prosciutto, in ½-inch dice
2 tablespoons freshly chopped Italian parsley
8 lasagne strips, approximately 4 by 12 inches

NOTE

A light tomato sauce can be served with this. Use Tomato Sauce with Butter on page 34 or Fresh Tomato Sauce on page 42.

the remaining lasagne strips. Cover with foil.

5. Bake for about 45 minutes. Remove from the oven and allow to cool for 20 or 30 minutes. Invert pie onto a serving platter and garnish with chopped parsley. To serve, slice as you would a cake or pie. Delicious!

VARIATIONS
To the filling, add ½ pound cooked, drained, and buttered pasta. Instead of lining the baking dish with lasagne strips, use large swiss chard leaves (parboiled and drained) arranged with plenty of leaf hanging over to encase fully the pasta rustica; or use lightly sautéed eggplant slices (cut lengthwise, not skinned, but ends removed).

WINE
A barbera del Monferrato or other robust red wine

Zucchini and Ziti Loaf with Chicken

1. Make the chicken filling first. In a bowl, combine chicken breasts and lemon juice. Allow to sit for 15 minutes.

2. In a skillet large enough to contain breasts in 1 layer, place chicken, garlic, celery, peppercorns, parsley, and salt and add enough water to cover. Bring to a boil, lower the heat, and simmer for 6 minutes, depending on thickness of breasts. Turn off heat, let chicken sit in water for 4 or 5 minutes, then remove from the liquid and cut in 1-inch pieces. Set aside. Discard or reserve liquid and vegetables for another use.

3. Heat butter in the small skillet, add the chicken pieces, and sauté for 1 minute. Add the brandy and cook for an additional minute. Add the cream and cook for 2 minutes more. Add the rosemary and turn off the heat. In a blender or food processor, add one-quarter of the chicken mix-

SERVES 6 TO 8

INGREDIENTS

2 cups small ziti, pasta shells, or fusilli
1/2 cup freshly grated parmesan or romano cheese
8 thick slices (1/2 inch) fresh tomatoes
2 tablespoons butter
1 tablespoon chopped fresh basil, or 1 teaspoon dried
chopped fresh parsley or spring onions for garnish
salt
freshly ground black pepper

ture. Purée for a few seconds and repeat blending or processing procedure until all the chicken is puréed.

4. In the meantime, have a large skillet ready for the zucchini and heat 3 tablespoons of butter. Sauté the zucchini for 2 or 3 minutes, add the shallots, onion, and garlic, and sauté for 2 minutes. Add the parsley and transfer the zucchini mixture to a large bowl.

5. In the same skillet, add the remaining 2 tablespoons of butter over medium-high heat. Add the mushrooms and sauté for 2 minutes. Add the vermouth and allow it to cook down for 2 or 3 minutes. Transfer the mushrooms to the zucchini mixture and set aside.

6. Bring 2 quarts of water to a rapid boil. Cook pasta for 5 minutes or so, depending on size of pasta, until it is *al dente*. Drain pasta and return it to the pan in which it cooked. Add the parmesan cheese and salt and pepper to taste and toss well.

7. Preheat the oven to 375 degrees. Liberally butter a 9 by 5-inch loaf pan. Add the chicken and zucchini mixtures to the pasta. Toss well and transfer to loaf pan. Cover with aluminum foil. Bake in oven for 40 minutes. Remove from the oven and allow to cool for 15 minutes. Use a small sharp knife to go around the perimeter of the loaf pan to loosen the edges.

8. While pasta form is resting, heat the remaining 2 tablespoons of butter in a skillet and sauté the tomato slices for 2 or 3 minutes on each side. When ready, place a large serving platter upside down over the loaf pan and invert to release the brick form. Arrange the tomato slices around the form, sprinkling the tomatoes with basil. Garnish with chopped

CHICKEN FILLING
3 whole chicken breasts, boned, skinned, and cut in half
juice of ½ lemon
1 clove garlic, unpeeled, cut in half lengthwise
1 stalk celery with leaves, chopped coarse
4 whole peppercorns
3 sprigs fresh parsley
1 teaspoon salt
2 tablespoons butter
3 tablespoons brandy
¾ cup heavy cream
1 tablespoon fresh rosemary; or 1 teaspoon dried, rubbed in palms of hands

ZUCCHINI FILLING
5 tablespoons butter
4 or 5 small zucchini, washed and grated coarse (3 cups)
½ cup finely chopped shallots
½ cup finely chopped onion
4 cloves garlic, chopped fine
3 tablespoons finely chopped fresh parsley
1 cup sliced mushrooms
3 tablespoons dry vermouth

parsley or spring onions. Slice at table and serve.

NOTE
This special pasta dish may be prepared ahead up to baking step. Make it the day before, refrigerate it overnight, then take it out of the refrigerator 1 hour before baking. Whenever possible, use fresh herbs. Two cups of canned Italian plum tomatoes could be sautéed in the butter if fresh red tomatoes are not available, prepared as a sauce around the brick, not over it.

WINE
A white sauvignon or other dry wine

Baked Ziti with Ricotta and Sausage

1. In a medium saucepan, melt 4 tablespoons of the butter, and add the flour. Stir and blend with a wire whisk and cook over medium heat for about 2 minutes. Slowly add the scalded chicken stock and wine and keep whisking. Allow the sauce to simmer for about 15 minutes. Set aside.

2. In a medium bowl, combine the ricotta with half the asiago cheese, beaten egg, 1 tablespoon of parsley, and salt and pepper to taste. Mix well and set aside.

3. In a medium skillet, heat the oil and sauté the sausage over medium-high heat for a few minutes or until done. Set aside.

4. Preheat the oven to 350 degrees. Cook the ziti for 5 minutes, no longer. Drain and return to the pot in which they cooked. Add the remaining tablespoon of butter and toss lightly.

SERVES 4

INGREDIENTS

5 tablespoons butter
1/2 cup all-purpose flour
2 cups chicken stock, heated
   with 1 cup white wine
1 pound ricotta
1 cup freshly grated asiago
   cheese
1 egg, lightly beaten
2 tablespoons finely chopped
   fresh parsley
1 teaspoon salt
freshly ground black pepper
2 tablespoons olive oil
2 links Italian sausage,
   casings removed and meat
   broken into small pieces
1/2 pound ziti

5. Butter a 2½- or 3-quart casserole or baking dish. Add one-fourth of the cooked ziti and spoon one-third of the sauce, and one-third of the ricotta mixture. Repeat the procedure ending with the ziti on top. Sprinkle the sausage and remaining parsley overall. Cover loosely with foil and bake for 35 to 40 minutes. Uncover the last 10 minutes. Pass remaining grated cheese.

WINE
A valtellina, such as valgella, or other dry red wine

Zucchini and Whole-wheat Pasta Pie

An easy and tasty pasta pie.

1. Put the zucchini into a bowl, add 2 teaspoons of salt, and let stand for 20 minutes to drain off the liquid. Take a tea towel and put the zucchini into it, roll it up and twist it to remove the moisture.

2. Preheat the oven to 350 degrees. In a large bowl place the zucchini, egg yolks, onion, mozzarella and romano cheeses, cooked pasta, milk, cream, basil, garlic, and salt and pepper to taste. Mix well and pour into a buttered 9- or 10-inch pie plate or quiche pan. Beat the egg whites until stiff and spoon onto the top.

SERVES 6

INGREDIENTS

1 pound zucchini, peeled and
coarsely grated
salt
3 eggs, separated
1 onion, chopped
¼ cup freshly grated
mozzarella cheese
¼ cup freshly grated romano
cheese
1 cup whole-wheat pasta,
cooked al dente
½ cup milk
½ cup light cream
1 tablespoon fresh basil, or 1
teaspoon dried
1 large clove garlic, chopped
fine
salt to taste
freshly ground black pepper

3. Bake pie in oven for 30 or 35 minutes or until nicely browned and a knife comes out clean. Slice and serve.

WINE

A cabernet from Lombardy, or other dry, medium-bodied red wine

Fettuccine with Chicken and Two Sauces

This tasty baked dish combines pasta with chicken and 2 sauces—one a garlic cream and one a simple fresh tomato sauce. A broader string pasta such as fettuccine is good here but other types may be used.

1. Wash the chicken and put it in a covered saucepan. (The saucepan shouldn't be much larger than the chicken.) Add the neck, gizzard, and heart. Add the celery, carrot, onion, salt, peppercorns, and dry vermouth, and cover with water. Bring to a boil, then lower the heat and simmer for 40 to 50 minutes, or until the chicken is cooked. (Do not overcook.) Transfer the chicken to a bowl or plate to allow it to cool.

SERVES 4 TO 6

INGREDIENTS

1 chicken (4 to 5 pounds) including neck, gizzard, and heart
2 stalks celery including green leaves, coarsely sliced
1 carrot, sliced thin
1 medium onion stuck with 2 cloves
1 teaspoon salt
10 cracked peppercorns, or ½ teaspoon ground
½ cup dry vermouth (optional)
1 pound fettuccine, preferably homemade
1 tablespoon butter
2 cups Tomato Sauce (page 34)
¾ cup freshly grated parmesan cheese
4 tablespoons finely chopped scallions, including green parts

2. As soon as you can handle the chicken (the sooner, the better), remove all the meat from the bones. Discard the skin and other fatty parts, but return all the bones to the stockpot. Boil the stock rapidly to let it cook down to about 2½ cups. Meanwhile, cut the chicken pieces into chunks of 1 to 2 inches, and set aside.

3. Next prepare the garlic cream sauce. Melt the butter in a saucepan. Add the garlic pieces and cook until they begin to turn golden; do not allow them to brown. Add the flour, and cook for about 2 minutes. Slowly add 2 cups of hot chicken stock, and cook over low heat for about 20 minutes.

4. In a small bowl, beat the egg yolk, cream, and red pepper flakes. Add the remaining ½ cup of hot stock to this mixture, beat well, and then add this cream sauce to the sauce in the pan. Keep the sauce warm; you will have about 3 cups of sauce.

5. Preheat oven to 350 degrees. Cook the pasta until *al dente.* Drain and return to the pot in which it cooked. Add butter to the pasta and toss lightly. With the aid of a rubber spatula, add half the cream sauce to the pasta.

CREAM GARLIC SAUCE
2 tablespoons butter
*1 large clove garlic, chopped
    very fine*
*4 tablespoons all-purpose
    flour*
1 egg yolk
¾ cup heavy cream
pinch of red pepper flakes

6. Transfer half of this mixture to a buttered oval baking dish about 14 by 9 inches. Add half the tomato sauce and all the chicken. Add the remaining pasta and cover with the remaining tomato sauce. Top with the remaining cream sauce. Sprinkle the cheese and chopped scallions overall. Bake in oven for 20 to 25 minutes, until the entire dish is well heated and the top is lightly browned.

WINE
A spanna (nebbiolo) or other dry, medium-bodied red wine

Pasta in an Eggplant Mold

A delicious, sophisticated dish.

1. Cut off the top and bottom ends of the eggplant (it should be able to sit upright) and slice lengthwise into very thin slices. Do not peel. Freely salt each slice and put them in a colander to drain for 1 hour. Discard any liquid; it is bitter and has no use. Pat dry each slice and set aside.

2. Heat enough vegetable oil in a deep-fryer (there should be about 3 inches of oil) until hot enough to deep fry eggplant slices (about 325 degrees). Deep-fry them, several at a time, until well done—golden. This will take about 3 minutes, 1½ for each side. When done, remove with tongs to paper toweling to drain.

SERVES 6 TO 8

INGREDIENTS
1 eggplant, about 1 pound
vegetable oil for deep-frying
1½ cups Tomato Sauce with
*   Vegetables (page 35)*
½ pound small pasta such as
*   bows, shells, penne, elbows,*
*   cooked al dente*
4 large eggs, hard-cooked,
*   peeled, and chopped coarse*
½ pound fontina, cut into
*   ¼-inch cubes*
salt
freshly ground black pepper
3 tablespoons freshly grated
*   parmesan cheese*
2 tablespoons butter

3. Preheat oven to 375 degrees. In a large bowl, combine the tomato sauce, cooked pasta, eggs, fontina cheese, and salt and pepper to taste. Set aside.

4. Liberally butter a 2½-quart ceramic soufflé dish and line it with half the eggplant slices. With a large spoon, transfer the pasta mixture to the soufflé dish. Cover with the remaining eggplant slices. Sprinkle the parmesan over the top and dot overall with butter. Bake for 30 minutes, until heated through and bubbling.

WINE
A gattinara or other robust red wine

142

Duck Lasagne with Porcini and Truffles

This is an unusual, but spectacular lasagne dish. It is quite delicate tasting. Make the lasagne strips as thin as possible, and have a few extra strips in case some break while cooking and draining. Served in small portions, this will make an excellent and unusual first pasta course.

1. Soak the mushrooms in the sherry for 1 hour, or until they swell to original size.

2. Cook 6 strips of lasagne pasta for 4 minutes. Drain in colander *which sits in another pan in order to catch the water for reuse.* Carefully transfer each strip to cotton kitchen toweling and pat dry. Boil the same cooking water again and cook 6 more strips. Drain and pat dry and cook until all pasta is done.

3. Preheat the oven to 350 degrees. To assemble and bake, use a baking dish 9 by 11 inches or 12 inches oblong, 2 inches deep. Put

SERVES 12

INGREDIENTS

1 cup finely chopped porcini (dried Italian mushrooms)
1/2 cup dry sherry
24 lasagne strips
6 cups rich duck stock
2 cups chopped duck meat
1 large black truffle (1 inch thick), cut into julienne strips, 1/2 inch by 1/16 inch
3/4 cup grated parmesan cheese
4 tablespoons butter, in 1/2-inch pieces

a little stock in the bottom of the baking dish and lay 3 strips of pasta at a time slightly overlapping lengths. There will be about 7 or 8 layers of pasta. Over each layer pour some stock, then add some duck meat, parmesan cheese, and mushrooms. After 4 layers, add some truffles. Add remaining truffles to the top layer. Dot with butter every other layer.

4. Cover with foil, and bake for 30 to 40 minutes. Let stand 10 minutes before serving.

NOTE

To make duck stock, use a 3 to 4 pound duck, cut up in quarters. Allow to cool just to a point of handling it, then remove enough breast, thigh, and leg meat and dice.

WINE

A chianti classico or other dry, medium-bodied red wine

Lasagne with Veal and Tarragon

A different way to prepare lasagne, with the magnificent flavor of veal and tarragon.

1. Cook the lasagne strips until less than *al dente*. Do not overcook; the pasta will cook some more in the oven. Lay the strips on cotton kitchen toweling and pat them dry with kitchen toweling.

2. Preheat oven to 375 degrees. Arrange several pasta strips to completely cover the bottom of a 9½ by 13½-inch baking dish that is 2 inches deep. Cover this layer with some of the veal, mushrooms, stock, salt and pepper to taste, and cheese. Repeat with additional layers of pasta and add more of the other ingredients until all the lasagne strips, veal, mushrooms, stock, and cheese have been used.

SERVES 6 TO 8

INGREDIENTS
1 pound freshly made lasagne
1½ to 2 cups julienned cooked veal
1 pound fresh mushrooms, sliced finely, tossed in juice of 1 lemon
4 cups clarified veal and beef stock
salt
freshly ground white pepper
6 tablespoons grated parmesan cheese
1 tablespoon finely chopped fresh tarragon, or 1 teaspoon dried

3. Bake for approximately 30 minutes or until the pasta and sauce bubble strongly and the dish is heated thoroughly. Remove from the oven and sprinkle tarragon overall. If you're using dried, rub between your hands as they go over the top of the baked dish. This gives extra essence to the aroma of the tarragon.

NOTE
Use about 1 pound of veal cutlets (approximately 6 small cutlets) sautéed in 2 tablespoons of butter, cooled, and sliced in ¼-inch strips. Or cut ¼-inch strips, about 2 or 3 inches long, from slices of a roast veal, a leftover roast you may have on hand.

WINE
A full and fruity white wine such as pinot grigio

Bowtie and Spinach Soufflé

1. In a medium saucepan, melt the butter. Add the shallots, and sauté until tender, about 2 minutes. Add the flour all at once, and mix well. Gradually add the milk, stirring constantly and cook until the sauce is thickened. (It should have the consistency of thin mayonnaise.) Add the nutmeg, salt, and pepper to taste. Cover the sauce with a piece of foil or wax paper and let it cool slightly.

2. In the meantime, preheat the oven to 400 degrees. Place the oven rack on the second shelf from the bottom. Beat the egg yolks lightly and add them to the sauce and mix until very smooth. Then add the spinach and set aside.

3. Cook the bowties in boiling water for about 4 or 5 minutes; do not *overcook*. Drain the bow-

SERVES 5 TO 6

INGREDIENTS

¼ cup butter
¼ cup finely chopped shallots
¼ cup all-purpose flour
1⅓ cups milk
¼ teaspoon freshly grated nutmeg
1 teaspoon salt
freshly ground black pepper
4 eggs, at room temperature, separated
1 cup chopped fresh spinach, or 1 package (10 ounces) frozen, cooked briefly
2 cups bowtie pasta
1 cup freshly grated asiago cheese
1 cup chopped fontina cheese

ties and add them to the spinach and sauce. Add the asiago and the fontina cheeses. Mix well, but gently.

4. Beat the egg whites until stiff, but not dry. Gently fold about one-quarter of the egg whites into the bowtie mixture. Transfer the remaining mixture to a buttered 2-quart soufflé dish or baking dish. Cover the top of the mixture with the rest of the egg whites. Place in the oven and reduce the heat to 375 degrees.

5. Bake 35 to 40 minutes until top is a golden brown or until a skewer inserted into the center of the soufflé comes out clean. Serve within 5 minutes.

WINE
A white sauvignon or other dry wine

Fettuccine Soufflé with Sausage and Two Cheeses

Fennel, fontina, and fettuccine combine here for one of the best dishes in this book.

1. Cook the fettuccine until *al dente;* do not overcook. Drain the pasta and return it to the pot in which it was cooked.

2. Preheat the oven to 350 degrees. Add the milk and mix a little. Add the butter, fontina and parmesan cheeses, sausage, fennel seeds, and salt and pepper to taste. Let the mixture cool, add the egg yolks and mix thoroughly.

SERVES 6

INGREDIENTS
½ pound green fettuccine
1⅔ cups milk, heated until small bubbles appear on top
9 tablespoons butter
4½ ounces fontina cheese, grated
¼ cup freshly grated parmesan cheese
½ pound Italian sweet sausage, casing removed and meat chopped fine and sautéed briefly
½ teaspoon dried fennel seed
6 large eggs, separated (at room temperature), yolks lightly beaten
salt
freshly ground black pepper

3. In a medium bowl, beat the egg whites until stiff but not dry. Fold the egg whites into the fettuccine mixture. Turn the mixture into a 3-quart soufflé dish or casserole and bake for 30 minutes. Turn the oven up to 375 degrees and bake for 10 minutes more. Let sit for 10 minutes before serving.

WINE
A pinot grigio or pinot blanco

STUFFED PASTAS

S tuffing foods of all kinds has universal appeal, but it is in Italian cookery that one sees the most creative combinations of one food stuffing another. Pasta is the most frequent recipient of stuffings and many shapes are famous world wide: ravioli, lasagne, tortellini, manicotti, canneloni, just to mention the more popular ones. Pasta is an ideal food for filling. It not only contains the filling easily and well (there *are* times when a ricotta filling will slip out of a ravioli container, but we never seem to mind that), but the pasta itself is a fine foil for the filling it receives. It adapts to many fillings and sauces in the same way as does basic pie pastry.

The string and ribbon pastas like spaghetti, the thinner spaghettini, flat linguine, and broad lasagne are reasonably easy to cope with. But how many of us know how to work with the popular manicotti and tufoli, or the pouch conchiglie (giant shells)? Actually, these are easy to prepare and need only be cooked in vast quantities in boiling, salted water until tender, then filled with a cheese, vegetable, or cooked meat stuffing. Layered or filled and baked with a previously prepared sauce, these make substantial meals. Unlike most other pastas, they can if necessary be prepared ahead and baked just before serving.

Pasta producers are extending the range of their products monthly; we can't go by the supermarket's pasta shelves without finding something new. Three of the basic ones are:

ANOLINI: These are small envelopes of pasta made of 2 pieces of pasta placed together, the filling consisting of bread crumbs, eggs, parmesan cheese, seasoning and concentrated beef stew. They are served in broth or dry with sauce.

AGNOLOTTI: This is a variety of stuffed envelopes of pasta of which ravioli is the best known. Traditionally, stuffed pasta should only be called "ravioli" when it is stuffed with eggs, ricotta, and other cheeses. When the small squares of pasta are stuffed with any of the meat fillings, such as chopped chicken, brains, salami, or spinach, they should be called "agnolotti."

CANNELLONI: These are numbered among the largest of the stuffed pasta of Italy. They are squares of pasta cooked in boiling, salted water then stuffed, rolled up, and browned in the oven. Sometimes they are baked with butter and sprinkled generously with parmesan cheese or, as in Tuscany, they are covered with a sauce and baked until the top is a golden brown.

Pasta Shells Stuffed with Chicken and Parsley

1. In a medium skillet or saucepan, cook the chicken breast in water with the celery, onion, and peppercorns. Simmer for 15 minutes, then remove the chicken and, when it is cool enough to handle, cut into small cubes, ¼ to ½ inch. This will make about 2 cups.

2. Put the chicken with 3 tablespoons of cream into the bowl of a food processor and process to a count of four. Transfer the chicken mixture to a large bowl and add the remaining cream, eggs, parsley, garlic, half the cheese, nutmeg, and salt and pepper to taste. Mix well.

SERVES 6

INGREDIENTS

1 whole boneless chicken breast
2 cups water
1 stalk celery with leaves, chopped coarse
1 very small onion, chopped coarse
4 peppercorns
6 tablespoons heavy cream
2 eggs, lightly beaten
4 tablespoons finely chopped parsley
1 clove garlic, finely chopped
½ cup freshly grated parmesan cheese
½ teaspoon freshly grated nutmeg
salt
freshly ground black pepper
20 jumbo pasta shells
3 cups Filetto Sauce (page 37)

3. Preheat the oven to 400 degrees. Cook the pasta shells until *al dente,* drain well, and pat dry. Spoon a little sauce on the bottom of an 8″ × 10″ baking pan or casserole. Fill each shell with the chicken mixture, and place the filled shells in the pan. Spoon the sauce evenly over the shells. Sprinkle the remaining cheese overall. Bake for 25 minutes, then serve hot.

WINE

A riesling from Colli Berici, or other dry white wine

Conchiglie with Three Fillings

Often we make these giant shells in large quantities for parties, and fill them with 3 different stuffings. The cheese filling is so easy to make because no cooking is required.

1. For the cheese filling: in a large bowl, combine the ricotta, parmesan cheese, garlic, salt, a liberal grinding of black pepper, and the egg yolks, 1 by 1, beating well after each addition. Then mix in the scallions, parsley, and mozzarella, and taste for seasoning. The filling should be quite definite in flavor; add more salt, pepper, and even more scallions, if necessary. Cover with plastic wrap or foil and refrigerate for at least an hour.

SERVES 12 TO 24

INGREDIENTS

6 dozen giant shells (conchiglie)
6 cups Marinara Sauce
   (page 43)
6 cups Balsamella Sauce
   (page 46)
2 cups freshly grated parmesan

CHEESE FILLING

1 pound ricotta
¼ cup freshly grated parmesan
¼ teaspoon finely chopped
   garlic
½ teaspoon salt
freshly ground black pepper
3 large egg yolks
2 tablespoons chopped scallions
1 tablespoon chopped Italian
   parsley
¼ pound mozzarella, diced

SPINACH AND MUSHROOM FILLING

6 tablespoons butter
½ cup finely chopped shallots
1 teaspoon finely chopped
   garlic

2. For the spinach and mushroom filling: in a large skillet, melt 4 tablespoons of butter. Add the shallots and garlic and, stirring frequently, cook for 5 minutes without letting them brown. Add the spinach, raise the heat, and cook, stirring constantly, until all the moisture in the skillet evaporates and the spinach begins to stick lightly to the pan. With a rubber spatula, transfer it into a large mixing bowl.

3. Melt the remaining butter in the skillet and add the mushrooms. Cook over moderate heat for 2 or 3 minutes until they begin to give off their liquid, then raise heat and rapidly boil away almost all their moisture. Transfer the mushrooms to the mixing bowl. Stir the mixture for a few minutes to cool it.

4. With a wooden spoon, beat in the eggs, 1 at a time. Stir in the parmesan cheese, prosciutto, mozzarella, salt, and some pepper. Taste for seasoning and add more salt and pepper if you think it needs it.

5. For the sausage and veal filling: in a large skillet, heat the oil, add the shallots, and cook over moderate heat for about 5 minutes, stirring frequently. When they just begin to color, add the sausage meat. Raise the heat and sauté until it has rendered most of its fat; the meat should turn a light brown. Add the veal, sauté for 3 to 4 minutes over high heat until it has turned from pink to brown, then transfer everything in the skillet into a sieve and drain the meat of all fat.

6. In a large bowl, soak the bread crumbs in the heavy cream for 3 or 4 minutes, and add the drained meat. Beat together with a wooden spoon until the mixture is fairly smooth, then beat in the eggs 1 at a time. Stir in the parsley, rosemary, lemon zest, salt, and some pepper. Taste for seasoning.

1 pound fresh spinach, cooked, drained, and chopped; or 2 packages (10 ounces each) frozen spinach, squeezed dry and chopped
½ pound mushrooms, chopped coarse
2 eggs
4 tablespoons freshly grated parmesan
⅛ pound prosciutto or other smoked ham, chopped coarse
¼ pound mozzarella, diced
½ teaspoon salt
freshly ground black pepper

SAUSAGE AND VEAL FILLING
2 tablespoons olive oil
¼ cup finely chopped shallots
½ pound sweet Italian sausages, casings removed and meat crumbled
½ pound ground lean veal
6 tablespoons fine bread crumbs
½ cup heavy cream
2 eggs
2 tablespoons chopped Italian parsley
½ teaspoon chopped fresh rosemary; or ¼ teaspoon dried rosemary, crumbled
½ teaspoon chopped lemon zest
½ teaspoon salt
freshly ground black pepper

7. Cook the shells until *al dente,* drain, and dry thoroughly in a linen towel. Stuff 24 shells with one of the fillings; stuff remaining with other 2 fillings.

8. Preheat oven to 350 degrees. Butter several large baking pans to hold all the shells, and place them in. Pour the marinara and balsamella sauces over the shells in each pan and sprinkle with 1 cup of cheese, reserving the remainder to pass at the table later. Bake pasta for 30 minutes or until sauce bubbles and pasta is heated through.

WINE
Depending on filling chosen, a tocai or other medium-bodied white wine for the cheese filling; a merlot or other medium-bodied red for the spinach filling; a ribolla or robust red for the sausage filling

Chicken and Pork Filling
for Tortellini/Cappelletti

Cappelletti are cut into squares and when folded, resemble peaked hats, which is exactly what the name means. Tortellini are cut into circles and, when folded, are semicircles.

1. In a 10-inch skillet, melt the butter until it becomes bubbly. Add the pork strips along with some salt and pepper. Cook for about 5 or 6 minutes, until meat browns on all sides. With a slotted spoon remove strips and cool.

2. Add the chicken strips to the skillet with a little more salt and pepper and brown them on both sides. Chicken cooks much faster than pork and will take only about 2 minutes. Remove with a slotted spoon and let cool.

3. When cooled, chop both the pork and chicken into the smallest cubes possible. Do not blend or put in the food processor, as they will become too puréed. They must be cut in small pieces

SERVES 4 TO 6

INGREDIENTS
1 tablespoon butter
1 ounce lean pork loin, cut
 into 1/3-inch strips
salt
freshly ground black pepper
2 ounces boned chicken
 breast, skin and fat
 removed, cut into 1/3-inch
 strips
1 tablespoon finely chopped
 prosciutto
1/2 cup ricotta
1 yolk from a small egg
1/4 cup freshly grated
 parmesan cheese
1/4 teaspoon nutmeg
3/4 pound fresh pasta dough
 (page 9)

as you mince onions or garlic. Put the chicken and pork pieces into a bowl and combine with the prosciutto pieces, ricotta, egg yolk, parmesan cheese, nutmeg, and salt and pepper to taste. Mix well.

4. Whichever method of pasta making you use, roll the dough as thin as possible. Cut into 1½-inch squares and put approximately ¼ teaspoon of filling in the center of each square. Moisten the edges of the dough and then fold the square in half diagonally across forming a triangle. Seal by pressing down firmly so the sides adhere. To form a cappelletto, bend the triangle around the index finger and press one corner over the other. Be sure the point is looking skyward. As you make them, place them on dry kitchen toweling and turn them every few hours until they dry evenly. In this way, they will keep at least 5 days or longer. Keep them separated, or they may stick. Allow to dry, then use.

Tortellini with Four Herbs

The tortellini cook quickly, and the herb sauce may be made well ahead of time, making this dish one of the easiest to prepare. Serve this as a companion with vitello tonnato and sliced fresh tomatoes for a true Italian feast.

1. Combine the olive oil with parsley, basil, dill, marjoram, garlic, and pepper to taste. Allow to marinate for about an hour for the oil to excite the herbs (or release herbal flavors).

2. Cook the tortellini until *al dente*. Drain well in a colander and put the pasta back in the pan in which it cooked. Add the herb mixture and cheese to the pan and toss well. Adjust salt seasoning. Transfer the pasta to an attractive serving platter. Sprinkle the scallions overall and serve.

On the preceding pages: Straw and Hay Pasta with Salmon (recipe on page 128); Potato Gnocchi with Fontina (recipe on page 82).

SERVES 4 TO 6

INGREDIENTS

¾ cup olive oil
⅓ cup finely chopped fresh parsley, or 1 tablespoon dried
8 finely chopped large fresh basil leaves, or 1 teaspoon dried
2 tablespoons finely chopped fresh dill, or 1 teaspoon dill weed
2 tablespoons finely chopped fresh marjoram, or 1 teaspoon dried
3 cloves garlic, finely chopped
freshly ground pepper
½ cup freshly grated parmesan cheese
1 pound Tortellini with Chicken and Pork Filling
salt
2 scallions, finely chopped

NOTE

An added touch which strengthens the flavor of cheese is to add ¼ cup chopped fontina along with the scallions.

WINE

A white sauvignon or other dry white wine

Tortellini in Cream Sauce

One of the best sauces for tortellini is one of the simplest, and one of the best fillings for this sauce is chicken and prosciutto. Follow the tortellini filling recipe on page 152, but instead of combining pork, chicken, and prosciutto, use 5 ounces of chicken and 4 tablespoons of prosciutto.

1. Cook the tortellini for about 10 minutes or until tender. Drain well and return the pasta to the pot in which it cooked.

2. Add the butter to the pasta and return to the stove over low heat. Using a wooden spoon, mix until butter is melted. Add the carrots and cream and cook for 2 or 3 minutes or until the cream has thickened slightly.

3. Add the cheese, salt, nutmeg, and pepper. Mix well. Sprinkle with fresh basil on top.

SERVES 2 TO 4

INGREDIENTS

½ pound tortellini
4 tablespoons butter, at room temperature
½ cup heavy cream
1 small carrot, sliced very thin
½ cup freshly grated romano or parmesan cheese
salt
freshly grated nutmeg
freshly ground black pepper
1 tablespoon fresh basil, or 1 teaspoon dried

NOTE

The carrot pieces should be cut in julienne pieces. However, these carrot slices should be thin enough to begin to curl. Remember that they too will be very *al dente* since they will cook only 2 or 3 minutes.

WINE

A white sauvignon or other dry wine

Cannelloni with Chicken, Chicken Livers, and Prosciutto

1. Melt 2 tablespoons of butter in a skillet and sauté the chicken until lightly browned. Remove the chicken and set aside. In the same skillet, sauté the chicken livers for 1 minute.

2. In a food processor or blender, process the chicken breasts, livers, and prosciutto until roughly blended. Transfer the mixture to a bowl and add the cheese and parsley, and mix well. Add half the balsamella sauce to the chicken mixture and mix well. Season to taste with salt and pepper.

3. Cook the pasta squares (you'll need about 14) for 1 minute and very carefully lay the squares on a tea towel. Pat each one dry.

SERVES 4

INGREDIENTS

4 tablespoons butter
1½ chicken breasts, skinned and boned
2 chicken livers, washed and fat removed
5 thin slices prosciutto
⅔ cup freshly grated parmesan cheese
1 tablespoon finely chopped parsley
1 cup Balsamella Sauce (page 46)
salt
freshly ground black pepper
¾ pound fresh pasta dough (page 9), cut for cannelloni

4. Preheat the oven to 375 degrees. Spoon 1 large tablespoon of the chicken mixture onto each square. Roll up tightly. Butter an 8 by 10-inch baking dish. Coat bottom lightly with sauce, then place the cannelloni side by side. Add the remaining sauce on top. Dot with butter. Bake for 20 minutes or until lightly browned and bubbly.

NOTE
You will have lots of pasta trimmings left over. Do not waste them; they're delicious cooked up briefly with butter and cheese, or milk, salt, and pepper.

WINE
A bardolino or other dry, light-bodied red wine

Spinach-stuffed Cumin Crespelle

1. Prepare the crespelle. In a large bowl, combine flour and milk; mix lightly.

2. In a small bowl, beat the eggs with the cumin and salt, and add it to the flour mixture. Add spinach and butter. Beat until smooth. Let rest for at least 1 hour. When ready to use, mix again.

3. Heat a 5- or 6-inch skillet. Butter the pan lightly with a small brush or folded paper towel dipped into melted butter. Make sure the sides of the pan are buttered. Add ¼ cup of batter to the pan and very quickly rotate the pan, this way and that, to make sure the bottom of the pan is completely covered. Cook for 1 or 2 minutes, then using a small stainless paring knife to lift the edge slightly, with your hands turn it over and cook the other side for 1 or 2 seconds. Repeat the same procedure until all the batter is used up. Place each crespo on a sheet of wax paper and cover with

SERVES 6

INGREDIENTS

1 cup all-purpose flour
1 cup milk
2 large eggs, lightly beaten
1 tablespoon ground cumin
½ teaspoon salt
½ cup chopped fresh spinach; or 1 package (10 ounces) frozen, cooked briefly, drained, and chopped
3 tablespoons butter, melted and cooled

FILLING

½ tablespoon butter
4 shallots, chopped fine
2 cups Balsamella Sauce (page 46)
1 cup diced fontina cheese
1 teaspoon cumin seed

WINE

A riesling from Friuli or other medium-bodied white wine

a cloth until ready to use. This batter will make about 16 crespelle, but you will fill and serve only 12. Set aside.

4. In a medium saucepan over medium-high heat place the butter for the sauce and add the shallots. Sauté briefly; do not let the shallots brown. Add sauce and blend well. Strain sauce through a fine sieve. You should have 2 cups. Cover and set aside for no longer than ½ hour.

5. Preheat the oven to 400 degrees. Place the crespelle on a flat surface and into the center of each one, place 1 heaping tablespoon of fontina and a big pinch of cumin seed. Ladle 1 or 2 tablespoons of the sauce on top. Roll up and place the crespelle in a large, buttered baking dish. Add more sauce and top with remaining cheese.

6. Bake for 10 minutes or until nicely browned. Serve as an appetizer, 2 on each serving dish.

Crespelle with Chicken and Almonds

1. Prepare crespelle. Place chicken in bowl, and add lemon juice. Toss well; let stand 10 to 15 minutes. Preheat oven to 350 degrees.

2. Melt 1½ tablespoons of butter in a saucepan, and add the onion. Cook, stirring, until the onion is softened. Sprinkle with flour, and cook for 2 minutes, stirring with a wire whisk. Slowly add stock; stir rapidly. When thick and smooth, add half the cream. Simmer 10 minutes, stirring occasionally. Add fontina; add salt and pepper to taste.

3. Melt 1 teaspoon of butter in a small iron skillet (or some other suitable oven pan), and add the almonds in 1 layer. Place in oven and bake, shaking the skillet and stirring the almonds until they are golden brown. Remove and cool. Do not turn the oven off.

4. Drain the chicken pieces, pat them dry, and sprinkle them with salt and pepper to taste. Melt 2 tablespoons of butter in a skillet, and add the chicken. Brown on both sides quickly (about 3 to 4 minutes); remove. Add vermouth and cook about 30 seconds, stirring. Pour drippings into a bowl.

5. Cut the chicken into ½-inch cubes and add to the bowl. Add one-quarter of the cheese sauce, almonds, remaining cream, egg, ricotta, 4 tablespoons of parmesan cheese, and chopped parsley. Blend well.

6. Preheat the oven to 350 degrees. Spoon an equal amount of the chicken mixture down the center of each crespo; roll to enclose the filling. Select a large baking dish. Spoon enough sauce into the dish to cover the bottom, then arrange the crespelle over the sauce, and cover with a second layer of sauce. Cover the dish with foil and bake for 15 to 20 minutes, until bubbling. Sprinkle with remaining cheese, and glaze under the broiler. Sprinkle with lemon zest, and serve hot.

SERVES 6

INGREDIENTS
12 Crespelle (page 24)
2 chicken breasts, skinned, boned, and halved
juice of ½ lemon
3½ tablespoons plus 1 teaspoon butter
¼ cup finely chopped onion
2 tablespoons flour
1 cup rich chicken stock
½ cup heavy cream
½ cup grated fontina cheese
salt and black pepper
3 tablespoons slivered almonds
1 tablespoon dry vermouth
1 small egg
1 cup ricotta
6 tablespoons freshly grated parmesan cheese
3 tablespoons minced parsley
½ teaspoon minced lemon zest

WINE
A chianti classico or other medium-bodied red wine

Cold Lasagne Rolls with
Rice, Spinach, and Sausage

This recipe is for 12 rolls; 2 more lasagne strips are added in the event any strip breaks during cooking.

1. Heat the oil in a large skillet and cook the sausage links until well done. Remove the pan from the heat and transfer the sausage to a cutting board. Remove casing and put the sausage meat in a large mixing bowl. Discard the grease from the skillet (but do not wipe clean) and return it to the heat.

2. Add the onion to the skillet and sauté until it becomes limp, in three minutes or so. Add the mushrooms and sauté an additional 2 minutes; add the garlic and cook one minute more. Empty the contents of the skillet into the mixing bowl with the sausage.

SERVES 12

INGREDIENTS

1 tablespoon olive oil
2 links Italian sausage, sweet or hot
1 onion, chopped fine
¼ pound fresh mushrooms, sliced fine and cut in half
1 clove garlic, minced
1 cup rice, preferably Italian but long-grain may be used
½ finely diced fontina cheese
½ cup heavy cream
2 cups finely chopped fresh spinach (about ½ pound)
freshly ground black pepper
salt
14 lasagne strips, each measuring about 2¾ inches wide and 11½ inches long

3. Cook the rice in 2½ cups of water. Bring it to a boil, reduce the heat, cover, simmer, and stir it occasionally. In 15 to 20 minutes most of the water will be absorbed. Test the rice for doneness. Drain it and return it to the pan in which it cooked. Add the fontina pieces while the rice is hot and stir until the cheese is well combined with the rice. Transfer this to the mixing bowl.

4. Add the cream and spinach to the mixing bowl and fold until well combined. Add freshly ground pepper and test for salt seasoning. Set aside.

5. Combine ingredients for the sauce in a mixing bowl, mix well, and set aside.

6. Cook the lasagne strips until *al dente*. Drain into a colander and transfer the strips to kitchen towels (do *not* use paper—use cloth) and pat them dry. Place enough filling on each pasta strip to cover it entirely. Filling should be spread evenly to achieve about ⅓-inch thickness. Roll and place, seamside down, on a platter, a tray, 2 plates or whatever will fit into the refrigerator. Allow to cool for 30 minutes or so.

7. To serve on individual plates, slice each roll into thirds, placing *cut* side up. Overlap each slice in a straight line. Add about 4 tablespoons of sauce to each serving. Put 2 tablespoons of sauce over the slices and 2 alongside.

SAUCE

3 large ripe tomatoes, blanched, cored, peeled, and cut into ½-inch cubes
1 cup olive oil
⅓ cup white wine vinegar
1 teaspoon fennel seeds
1 teaspoon sugar
salt
freshly ground black pepper

The flavor is enhanced if the pasta slices are not too cold; room temperature or a bit cooler brings out more flavor. To serve on a large platter for buffet, cut each roll into 3 slices and overlap in a straight line, pouring some sauce on the slices and some alongside.

VARIATION
Make the lasagne rolls of Carrot kasta (page 54) and fill with a stuffing made with ¼ pound prosciutto instead of sausage, and swiss chard in place of spinach.

WINE
A valtellina, such as grumello, or another full-bodied red wine

Piselli Lasagne With Ricotta Filling

1. Prepare sauce. In a large saucepan, heat the olive oil and add the sausage meat. Sauté briefly, about 2 minutes, then add the shallots and garlic and sauté for 1 minute more. Add the tomatoes, basil, and sugar. Bring to a fast boil, lower heat, and simmer for 40 minutes. Stir frequently. Add salt and pepper to taste.

2. Cook 4 sheets of pasta at a time. Cook for 1 or 2 minutes or until nearly tender. Have another large saucepan ready with a colander placed on top of it, then carefully empty the boiling water and lasagne strips from the first saucepan through the colander into the second saucepan, catching the cooked pasta in the colander. Save the water for more uncooked pasta. Run the cooked pasta under cold water and lay it on a tea towel and pat dry. Cook the remaining lasagne strips, 4 sheets at a time, until all are cooked. Set aside.

SERVES 6 TO 8

INGREDIENTS

16 to 18 lasagne strips (page 19), 2 inches wide and 10 inches long, with extras if needed
1 cup Balsamella Sauce (page 46)
1 cup shredded fontina cheese
½ cup freshly grated parmesan cheese

RICOTTA FILLING

2 cups ricotta
1 tablespoon finely chopped fresh parsley
2 eggs, lightly beaten
½ teaspoon sugar
freshly ground black pepper

3. Combine ingredients for filling in a bowl and mix until smooth. Set aside.

4. Preheat the oven to 350 degrees. Select a baking pan 12 by 9 inches and 3 inches deep, or a round pan about 10 inches wide. Spoon a small amount of the tomato sauce into the bottom of the pan, then arrange 4 sheets of cooked pasta over the sauce. Add one-third of the ricotta mixture evenly overall, then one-third of the balsamella sauce and one-third of the fontina. Sprinkle 1 tablespoon of parmesan cheese and a small amount of the tomato sauce overall.

5. Cover with 4 more sheets of cooked pasta and repeat the procedure 2 more times, ending up with the cooked pasta on top. Cover with the more tomato sauce and sprinkle with the remaining parmesan cheese. Bake for 50 minutes or until bubbles appear around the edges. Let the lasagne set for 20 minutes before serving.

TOMATO SAUCE

2 tablespoons olive oil
1 pound Italian sweet sausage, casings removed and meat crumbled
2 shallots, chopped fine
1 large clove garlic, chopped fine
1½ pounds ripe plum tomatoes, peeled, cored, seeded, and chopped; or 1 can (2 pounds, 3 ounces) imported Italian plum tomatoes, puréed in a food mill
2 tablespoons finely chopped fresh basil, or 1 teaspoon dried
½ teaspoon sugar, if using fresh tomatoes
1 teaspoon salt
freshly ground black pepper

NOTE

This dish can be made up to a day ahead of time and kept in the refrigerator. Remove 1 hour before baking. Lasagne also freezes beautifully; wrap it well in foil and when ready to bake, no thawing is necessary. Cover with a fresh piece of foil and bake 350 degrees for 1½ hours. Remove foil after one hour and bake uncovered until lasagne is bubbling.

WINE

A chianti classico or other dry, medium-bodied red wine

Potato Gnocchi Roll

This is a spectacular party dish—light, lovely, tasty, and sure to please.

1. Place puréed potatoes in a medium bowl and add butter; mix until melted. Add the whole egg, 1 cup flour, nutmeg, ½ teaspoon of salt, and a pinch of pepper; mix well and form into a ball. Wrap and chill for about ½ hour.

2. In a bowl, mix spinach, ricotta, remaining butter, beaten eggs, cheese, remaining flour, and salt and pepper to taste.

3. Sprinkle some flour onto a large piece of wax paper. Roll dough out into a 9 by 12-inch rectangle (use a little more flour, if necessary). Spread filling over dough, leaving a 1-inch border on all sides. Fold over the bare edgings on 2 long sides and 1 short. Roll up dough from open short end as you would a jellyroll. Press in edges to seal.

SERVES 4 TO 6

INGREDIENTS

3 large Idaho potatoes, baked, peeled, and puréed
2 tablespoons butter
3 eggs, 2 lightly beaten together
1 cup plus 2 tablespoons all-purpose flour
pinch of freshly grated nutmeg
1½ teaspoons salt
freshly ground black pepper
½ cup freshly cooked spinach, drained, squeezed dry, and minced; or 1 package (10 ounces) frozen spinach, cooked, drained, and squeezed dry
1⅓ cups ricotta
¼ cup freshly grated romano cheese
Ragù Bolognese (page 39)

4. Very carefully wrap roll in clean white cloth. Tie ends tightly with kitchen string. Secure middle of the wrap with a large safety pin. Wrap again in cheesecloth. Secure ends with 2 safety pins. This is a fragile pasta roll and the 2 wrappings are security measures to prevent an opening.

5. Put the wrapped roll into a large heavy pan, approximately 13 by 14 inches. Add enough water to cover the roll. Cover and simmer for 1 hour and 30 minutes. Remove the roll. (You will need pot holders for this.) Remove the cloth and the cheesecloth and place the pasta roll carefully on a platter. Serve with the ragù bolognese.

WINE

A soave or other dry, medium-bodied white wine

Penne Wrapped in Phyllo

This makes a good appetizer or a wonderful luncheon dish.

1. In a small saucepan, melt 2 tablespoons of butter, add the shallots, and sauté briefly, about 2 minutes. Remove from heat.

2. In a bowl, add the penne, shallots, ricotta, fontina, parmesan, eggs, parsley, nutmeg, and salt and pepper to taste. Combine well.

3. Melt remaining butter over very low heat. Keep warm. Preheat the oven to 350 degrees.

4. On a large work surface, place 1 phyllo sheet and brush with the melted butter. Repeat until 5 sheets in all are buttered and stacked. Work fast; there is no need to cover the rest of the phyllo with a damp cloth if it is fresh. Spoon one-third of the pasta mixture along the short end of the layered phyllo closest to you; leave a ½-inch border on all sides. Top with 5 or 6 asparagus,

SERVES 6 TO 8

INGREDIENTS
1 cup plus 2 tablespoons butter
1 cup finely chopped shallots
1 cup penne, cooked al dente
1 cup ricotta
1 cup coarsely grated fontina cheese
¼ cup freshly grated parmesan cheese
2 eggs, lightly beaten
1 tablespoon finely chopped fresh Italian parsley, or 1 teaspoon dried
¼ teaspoon freshly ground nutmeg
salt
freshly ground black pepper
20 fresh asparagus (not canned)
15 sheets phyllo pastry, preferably fresh

WINE
A soave or other dry, medium-bodied white wine

depending on size, and very carefully roll the phyllo. Fold in each edge, lengthwise, and continue to roll jellyroll fashion. As you are rolling, brush with a little more melted butter. The pasta roll will be about 10 inches long and about 3 inches wide.

5. Repeat the procedure with the remaining phyllo and filling and place the 3 phyllo rolls, seam-side down, on a large buttered baking tray. With a sharp knife or razor blade, make light indentation marks, on the diagonal, into each roll (as you would to bread). Be sure not to cut too deep or you will have the mixture coming out and it will not look very pretty. Bake for 35 to 40 minutes or until very golden. Let sit 15 to 20 minutes before serving.

NOTE
Penne wrapped in phyllo freezes beautifully for at least 1 to 2 months. If frozen, put into oven at 325 degrees for 50 minutes.

Filled Lasagne Rolls with Two Sauces

1. Cook 4 lasagne strips at a time until *al dente*. Transfer strips to cotton or linen kitchen towels, laying the strips flat and patting dry with more toweling. In removing strips from the boiling water, pour the entire contents of the pasta pot into a colander which has been set into another pan. The cooking liquid which has drained into the second pan can be brought to another boil quickly since the water is already hot. Repeat until all strips are cooked, drained, and dried.

2. Place about 3 tablespoons of filling on each strip and with a rubber spatula or knife, spread the filling along the strip as evenly as you can. Roll each strip as tightly as you can.

SERVES 6

INGREDIENTS

12 lasagne strips, approximately 2 inches wide and 10 inches long
2 cups Cheese Filling or Spinach and Mushroom Filling, or Sausage and Veal Filling (pages 150–51)
2 cups Marinara Sauce (page 43)
1½ cups Balsamella Sauce (page 46)
½ cup freshly grated parmesan cheese

3. Preheat the oven to 350 degrees. In a 9 by 12-inch baking dish, spoon several tablespoons of balsamella sauce lightly coating the bottom of the baking dish. Arrange the lasagne rolls in the dish, fitting them snugly side by side being sure the seamside is down.

4. Pour the tomato sauce overall and then spoon the remaining balsamella sauce by striating across the red sauce, like thin long clouds in the sky. Sprinkle parmesan cheese overall.

5. Cover lightly with foil and bake for 25 to 30 minutes. Remove the foil the last 10 minutes of baking. Pasta and sauce should be hot and bubbly.

WINE
A valpolicella or other dry, medium-bodied red wine

COLD PASTA
AND PASTA SALADS

*C*old pastas seem to be the rage in Roma, Milano, in all the places along the Italian Riviera. They've caught on in New York, Los Angeles, and San Francisco, too. It's easy to understand why. Often one of these dishes is enough for a main course, ideal at lunch time or for a Sunday supper. They are easy to make, can be made ahead, and can be added to easily—they "stretch" so it is easy to say, "yes, bring along your friend." Cold pasta salads have extended the Italian pasta repertoire in many directions: new combinations of food are brought together so that the adjectives "exciting," "fulfilling," "esoteric," are often heard. One caution: use the best ingredients and serve these dishes at room temperature to get the full taste.

There are several delights here: mixed salads where pasta is the main ingredient; these are fun shapes—farfalle, pasta wheels, penne, tubetti, and so on. Others are cold salads, combining spaghettini with shrimp and dill. Or the pasta is a filling for a vegetable—or the reverse, a vegetable filling for the pasta. We have filled whole tomatoes with orzo and crabmeat and we have used tomatoes, basil, and garlic to fill giant pasta shells. The vermicelli bird nests are scoops of pasta that form a nest when deep-fried in oil. They make good containers for most of the cool pasta preparations in this chapter.

Lastly, there is the cold timballe, multi-layers of crespelle and mortadella sauced with tuna blended into a homemade mayonnaise. Beautiful to look at and lovely to eat.

Pasta with Tomatoes and Mozzarella in a Salad

For a delightful variation, use smoked mozzarella.

1. Rub the bottom and sides of a wooden bowl (8 or 9 inches wide) with the garlic clove. Discard any remaining garlic or reserve for another use.

SERVES 4

INGREDIENTS

1 clove garlic
½ pound pasta shells or other small pasta, cooked al dente, drained well, and cooled slightly
3 large firm tomatoes, peeled and cut into quarters
1 fresh medium mozzarella, cut into ¼-inch cubes
12 large basil leaves, washed and chopped fine; or 1 teaspoon dried
1 small purple onion, sliced in thin rings
½ cup olive oil
½ teaspoon dried oregano
salt
freshly ground black pepper

2. To the bowl, add the pasta, tomatoes, mozzarella, most of the basil (save a little for garnish), onion rings, oil, oregano, and salt and pepper to taste. Toss well. Sprinkle more fresh basil on top.

WINE
A dolcetto or other dry, medium-bodied red wine

Penne with Carrots, Onions, and White Wine

This unusual combination of ingredients recalls the Greek influence on the Italian boot. It makes a delicious and healthful salad to be served any time of the year. We often have it as a main course.

1. Peel and cut the carrots into julienne pieces, ¼ inch thick by 2 inches long. Peel and cut the onions into ½-inch wedges. There should be approximately 3 cups of carrots and 2 of onions.

2. In a large saucepan, combine the carrots with the water, vinegar, wine, oil, herbs, and seasonings. Bring this to a boil, lower heat, cover, and simmer for about 5 minutes. Then add the onions and simmer for 5 minutes more. Both vegetables should be cooked, but firm. Remove from the heat and allow to cool.

SERVES 4 TO 6

INGREDIENTS
1 pound carrots
1 pound onions
½ cup water
¼ cup white wine vinegar
½ cup dry white wine
⅓ cup olive oil
1 teaspoon coriander seeds
*1 teaspoon finely chopped
   fresh fennel, or ½
   teaspoon dried fennel seeds*
*1 teaspoon finely chopped
   fresh thyme, or ½
   teaspoon dried thyme*
2 bay leaves
2 teaspoons salt
freshly ground black pepper
1 pound penne

3. Cook the pasta until *al dente,* drain, and cool slightly. Combine pasta with the vegetables and sauce. Add considerable black pepper and serve.

WINE
A pinot grigio or pinot blanco

Vermicelli Bird Nests

Pasta in various forms lends itself to deep frying. This recipe for bird nests makes an attractive container for pasta preparations, especially cold pastas and pasta salads. Although the bird nests are edible, they are very crunchy. Use them instead as a container as one might a sea shell.

1. Cook vermicelli just until *al dente*. (It is better to undercook this as it will cook again.) Drain well and return to pot in which it cooked. Add butter, herbs, salt, and pepper and toss well. Be sure each strand of pasta is coated as this will help prevent sticking.

2. Heat oil in a small, deep saucepan, approximately 6½ inches wide by 4 inches deep until it reaches 325 degrees. While oil is heating (watch carefully), arrange some of the cooked pasta in a basket spoon. Since a smaller sister basket spoon will be inset into the larger one, try to arrange the pasta in a well, so the smaller spoon will sit in it to form a basket

MAKES 6 NESTS

INGREDIENTS

½ pound vermicelli
2 tablespoons butter, softened
herbs as desired (see note)
salt
freshly ground black pepper
⅔ to ¾ quart corn or
   vegetable oil

NOTE

Different herbs and spices can be added to cooked vermicelli before forming them. For example, if you plan to use the tomato, basil and garlic filling (page 166), add about 1 tablespoon finely chopped fresh basil (or 1 teaspoon dried) to the vermicelli. Add some finely chopped celery leaves, about ⅓ cup of filling with the farfalle salad (page 169). Do not use garlic; however, onions or shallots are all right.

or nest form. Once this has been set (spoons together and clipped), cut off pasta ends with scissors—do this over pasta pan so cut ends are not wasted.

3. Immerse the basket spoon filled with pasta into the hot oil. When the pasta is submerged, the oil should bubble with great effervescence, especially at the beginning. The bubbling will subside somewhat but not much. Cook for 3 to 4 minutes and remove spoon. The pasta nest should be golden—not brown or scorched. Remove the clips on the basket spoon and then the smaller spoon. Turn over the large spoon and tap on a flat surface lined with 2 layers of paper toweling. The nest should release itself easily and, if by chance, it doesn't hold its shape, it didn't cook long enough. Repeat until 6 nests are made.

4. Fill each nest with any of the fillings on pages 166–171.

Farfalle Salad in Vermicelli Bird Nests

1. In a medium bowl, combine onion, olives, mushrooms, artichoke hearts, oil, vinegar, marjoram, and dill. Allow to sit for 2 or 3 hours. It is not necessary to refrigerate this.

2. Cook the farfalle until *al dente.* Drain well and transfer to a cloth kitchen towel. Pat dry and quickly put in a large mixing bowl.

On the preceding pages: Orange Pasta with Spinach Slivers, Mushrooms, and Cream (recipe on page 53); Whole-Wheat Pasta with Sausage and Fennel (recipe on page 69); Escarole and Pasta Soup (recipe on page 184); Pasta Timbale with Mortadella (recipe on page 176).

SERVES 6

INGREDIENTS

*1 small red onion, thinly
    sliced and separated into
    rings
1 cup pitted ripe olives
8 ounces fresh mushrooms,
    sliced thin
1 can (14 ounces) artichoke
    hearts, drained and
    quartered
6 tablespoons olive oil
2 tablespoons white vinegar
1 teaspoon finely chopped
    fresh marjoram, or ¹/₂
    teaspoon dried
1 teaspoon finely chopped
    fresh dill, or ¹/₂ teaspoon
    dried
8 ounces farfalle
1 cup diagonally sliced celery
1 cup halved cherry tomatoes
¹/₂ cup diced green pepper
¹/₂ cup freshly grated parmesan
salt
freshly ground black pepper
4 ounces mortadella, diced*

3. To the pasta in the bowl add the celery, tomatoes, green pepper, parmesan cheese, salt and pepper to taste, the marinated vegetables, and the cubes of mortadella. Toss lightly, but well. If the salad is made ahead and kept in the refrigerator, take it out 30 minutes before serving. Toss again before serving. Place salad in Vermicelli Bird Nests and serve.

WINE
A riesling from Friuli or any other dry, medium-bodied white wine

Pasta Wheels in a Sweet-Sour Salad

1. In a medium pot, cook the pasta for 5 or 6 minutes or until *al dente*. Drain it well by shaking the strainer or colander to be sure most of the water is removed.

2. Transfer the pasta to a large bowl and add the onion, green or red pepper, celery, carrot, chives, and parsley. Set aside.

3. In a medium bowl, combine the olive oil, vinegar, sugar, mayonnaise, sour cream, salt, and pepper. With a wire whisk, beat hard until very creamy. Pour over pasta and mix well. Correct seasoning if necessary.

SERVES 4

INGREDIENTS

2 cups pasta wheels (rotelle)
½ purple onion, chopped fine
¼ cup finely chopped green
   or red bell pepper
1 stalk celery including the
   leaves, chopped fine
1 small carrot, diced
2 tablespoons finely chopped
   fresh chives
1 tablespoon finely chopped
   fresh or frozen parsley
¼ cup olive oil
1 tablespoon white wine
   vinegar
1 teaspoon sugar
¼ cup mayonnaise,
   homemade if possible
¼ cup sour cream
1 teaspoon salt
freshly ground black pepper
parsley pieces or pepper strips
   for decoration

4. Cover the pasta salad with foil and refrigerate for a few hours, for the flavors to blend. Remove the salad from the refrigerator 30 minutes before serving.

5. To serve, mound the pasta salad on a pretty platter, and sprinkle some parsley on top, or decorate the top with pepper strips.

WINE
A trebbiano di romagna or other dry, light white wine

Tubetti and Gorgonzola Salad

1. Allow the gorgonzola to reach room temperature. Then put it in a bowl and mash it with a fork. Add the lemon juice, mustard, and cream and stir until blended but somewhat lumpy. Add the onion, prosciutto, and parsley and combine well. Season to taste with freshly ground pepper.

2. Cook the tubetti until *al dente,* drain well, and put in a large mixing bowl. Add the butter and coat the pasta. Add half the gorgonzola mixture, stir well, and set aside.

3. Cut the melon in half so the stem and opposite end are on the bottom. Remove the seeds with a spoon and, if desired, use a paring knife to remove the skin. Slice each half into ½-inch to 1-inch slices. These should be circular—like large flat doughnuts. Use only 4 or 6 of the larger slices and reserve the remainder for another purpose.

SERVES 4 TO 6

INGREDIENTS

⅓ pound gorgonzola
juice of ½ lemon
2 tablespoons Dijon-style
   mustard
½ pint heavy cream
1 small sweet red onion,
   chopped fine
¼ pound prosciutto, chopped
   fine
½ cup finely chopped fresh
   parsley
freshly grated pepper
½ pound tubetti
2 tablespoons butter
lettuce leaves (optional)
parsley sprigs
1 cantaloupe

4. If desired, arrange 2 or 3 lettuce leaves on each plate. Put a cantaloupe slice on the lettuce. Divide the pasta salad among 4 or 6 melon slices. Add a parsley sprig and pass the remaining gorgonzola sauce and a peppermill.

NOTE
You could also use melon halves. To serve 4, cut 2 melons in half so the stem and opposite ends are on the bottom. Remove the seeds and skin, and slice a piece from each bottom half so the melon half will sit upright. Cut a wedge from each half: fill the melon with the pasta salad and insert the wedge partially into the melon. Garnish with parsley and pass more gorgonzola sauce.

WINE
A sauvignon from Bologna or other dry white wine

Spaghettini with Shrimp and Dill

1. Combine all the ingredients, except the shrimp and spaghettini, and mix until well blended. Add the shrimp and allow to marinate for at least 30 minutes.

2. Cook the pasta until *al dente,* drain well, and return to the pan in which it cooked.

SERVES 4

INGREDIENTS
1/3 cup dry white wine
1/4 cup white wine vinegar
1 cup olive oil
*2 tablespoons finely chopped
   fresh dill, or 1 teaspoon
   dried*
2 teaspoons salt
freshly ground black pepper
*1 pound shrimp, shelled,
   deveined, cooked, and
   sliced in half lengthwise*
1 pound spaghettini

3. Add the sauce and toss well until each strand is coated. Serve in individual plates or in one large platter or bowl.

WINE
A soave or other medium-bodied white wine

Tomatoes Stuffed with Orzo and Crabmeat

1. Wash the tomatoes and remove each core. Scoop out some pulp and seeds and discard. Salt each tomato and turn upside down on a large platter. Drain their liquid (water) for about 30 minutes.

2. Meanwhile combine all other ingredients. Toss and taste for seasoning; add more salt and freshly ground pepper if necessary.

3. Turn the tomatoes and fill them with the crabmeat and pasta filling. Allow the filling to overflow the tomato, down one side. Sprinkle more freshly ground pepper on top. Serve at room temperature.

SERVES 6

INGREDIENTS
6 medium to large tomatoes
½ cup orzo, cooked, drained, and dried in cotton kitchen toweling
1 pound crabmeat, cooked and cooled
½ cup chopped spring onions, including tender green parts
1 small to medium cucumber, peeled, seeded, and cut into ¼-inch dice
2 tablespoons prepared horseradish
juice of 1 lemon
¾ cup olive oil
salt
freshly ground pepper

NOTE
You could substitute cooked filets of sole or cooked small shrimp. The fish should be mostly whole but if it breaks into several pieces, don't be concerned.

WINE
A pinot grigio or other light white wine

Pasta Stars and Asparagus Spears in Cucumber Boats

1. Salt the cucumber halves liberally, put them in a colander, and allow to drain for about ½ hour. Rinse off the salt and dry the cucumbers with kitchen toweling. Set aside.

2. Combine the oil and the mustard and mix until blended. Add the vinegar, shallots, and salt and pepper to taste in a bowl; mix well.

3. Measure out one-third of the dressing and marinate the asparagus in it for 15 to 20 minutes. Drain and reserve the marinade.

4. Add the remaining dressing to the cooked pasta. Toss well and spoon the pasta into the cucumber halves. Arrange 2 asparagus spears on each cucumber half. Spoon the reserved marinade over the asparagus.

SERVES 6

INGREDIENTS

3 cucumbers, ends trimmed then peeled, cut in half lengthwise, and scooped deeply
salt
¾ cup olive oil
¼ teaspoon Dijon-style mustard
¼ cup white wine vinegar
¼ cup finely chopped shallots
freshly ground pepper
½ cup pasta stars (stellini), cooked al dente and drained well
12 thin asparagus spears, cut to fit inside cucumber halves, then shaved, cooked al dente, and dried in kitchen toweling
2 tablespoons fresh chopped parsley

5. Serve immediately or refrigerate them until ready to serve. If refrigerated for later, remove from the refrigerator at least ½ hour before serving. Garnish with fresh chopped parsley.

WINE
An albano secco or other light, fresh white wine

Pasta Shells Filled With Tomato, Basil, and Garlic

1. Cook the pasta shells until *al dente*. Drain very well. After they are drained, transfer to cotton or linen kitchen toweling and pat dry. Set aside.

2. In a large bowl, combine the tomatoes, cucumber, basil, garlic, olive oil, vinegar, and salt and pepper to taste. Mix well.

SERVES 6 TO 8

INGREDIENTS
16 giant pasta shells
6 large ripe tomatoes, peeled, seeded, and chopped
1 medium cucumber, peeled, seeded, and cubed (¹/₄-inch)
8 leaves fresh basil, chopped fine
2 cloves garlic, peeled and chopped fine
²/₃ cup olive oil
¹/₄ cup sherry wine vinegar, or red or white wine vinegar
salt to taste
freshly ground black pepper

3. Fill each pasta shell evenly with the tomato mixture. Refrigerate until cool. Serve 2 pasta shells on each plate, paired with a fresh basil leaf. If you don't have fresh basil leaves, use lettuce, escarole, or other leaves or even a large parsley sprig.

WINE
A dolcetto or other dry, medium-bodied red wine

Pasta Timbale with Mortadella

This is a fairly rich dish, so small servings are in order. It is a show-stopper, especially good as an appetizer.

1. In a food processor, blend the tuna and anchovies until smooth. Add 1 cup mayonnaise and the lemon juice and process a little more. Transfer this to a large bowl.

2. Add remaining mayonnaise to tuna mixture and add some, or all of the chicken stock to achieve a consistency slightly thicker than heavy cream. Blend thoroughly until all is amalgamated.

3. In an 8-inch springform pan, place 1 crespo on the bottom and add enough mortadella slices to cover the entire surface of the crespo. Spoon a very thin coating of the tuna sauce over the mortadella.

SERVES 12 TO 20

INGREDIENTS

1 can (7 ounces) Italian tuna packed in olive oil
6 flat anchovy filets
2 cups mayonnaise, homemade if possible
juice of 1 lemon
1 cup cool chicken stock
16 8-inch Crespelle (page 24)
1 pound mortadella, sliced thin
3 tablespoons small capers
3 tablespoons finely chopped freshly parsley

4. Repeat this procedure until all crespelle are used. End with crespo on top. Refrigerate for several hours, or overnight.

5. Remove timbale from the refrigerator and then remove the springform. The crespelle will appear somewhat uneven; with a sharp knife, trim the edges to form as straight an edge as possible. Cover with additional sauce and sprinkle capers and parsley overall. Slice the timbale as you would a cake and serve with remaining sauce. (Put the sauce *on the side* of the slice, *not* over it.)

WINE
A valpolicella or bardolino

PASTA IN SOUPS

*I*n most Italian homes soup is a way of life, and it is eaten each day, all year long. There are three kinds of soup in Italy. One is minestrone, somewhat full and thick and laden with pasta (or rice) and lots of wonderfully fresh vegetables. The second is thinner, often clear and based on a chicken or beef broth; into these soups are added small pasta (little stars, orzo, angel's hair, and so on) or stuffed pastas such as ravioli and tortellini. These soups have a mystique and that's one reason why they are so exciting. The clear broth has a clear, warm taste and the pasta, especially if stuffed, is often an amazing surprise for who can guess the cook's fantasy of stuffing. Eggs and parsley? Breadcrumbs and black pepper? Meat and cheese? The third variety of soup is the magnificent fish soups, made all along Italy's coastlines. These *zuppe di pesce* do not contain pasta (or rice for that matter) but even without pasta, the traveler should have it on any trip to Italy.

Minestrone is probably the most well-known Italian soup. The word *minestra* is Italian for a thick soup. In days when inns were few and far between, travelers found shelter in monasteries. The monks, accustomed to receiving guests at all hours, would always have a cauldron of meat and vegetables simmering on the stove. *Minestra,* derived from the Latin *ministrare,* means "to serve." *Minestrone,* which means literally, a large minestra, is a soup of beef stock in which is cooked a combination of many vegetables and pastas with just enough stock to float both. In Italian households the meat which gives stock its flavor is usually left in the soup, thereby making the minestrone a one-course meal.

The soup of Small Shells, Chick Peas and Rosemary is a classic one from Tuscany, where the purest Italian is spoken and some of the purest classical food comes from. Events in Tuscany have been captured by artists and by cooks, for in Tuscany cooking is not just a passion, it is an art. In preparing dishes of this classic simplicity, the cook relies on skill alone and the excellence of beautiful raw materials. The only luxury in Tuscany is olive oil; it is there in Lucca, the center of the olive oil trade, from which comes some of the world's best olive oil.

In Italy, piping hot soups are served in summertime. Cold soups, although gaining in popularity, are not as frequently served in summer as they are in the U.S. But the Italian feeling is that if a hot soup warms the cockles of your heart in winter, it can surely cool them in the heat of summer for it provides insulation against the heat as well.

Minestrone

All the good things of Earth put together in 1 saucepan. It is Italian cuisine at its best.

1. Soak the beans in water to cover overnight and drain just before adding to the soup.

2. On the next day, heat the oil in a large souppot and sauté the onions and bacon. Add the garlic, marjoram, basil, and thyme and cook until the garlic just begins to turn color. Add the tomatoes and pour in the red wine. Let mixture come to a boil and add the drained beans.

3. Add 3 pints of hot water to the souppot, bring to a boil, turn down the heat, and let simmer steadily for 2 hours.

SERVES 6 TO 8

INGREDIENTS

*¼ pound dried beans—
  white, pink, or red kidney*
3 tablespoons olive oil
2 small onions, chopped coarse
2 slices bacon, 1-inch pieces
2 cloves garlic, chopped fine
½ teaspoon dried marjoram
½ teaspoon dried basil
½ teaspoon dried thyme
*4 fresh tomatoes, peeled,
  seeded, and chopped; or
  1½ cups chopped canned
  Italian plum tomatoes*
1 cup red wine
2 large carrots, in ½-inch pieces
1 small turnip, ½-inch cubes
1 stalk celery, ½-inch pieces
*½ small cabbage, in ½ by
  2-inch julienne pieces*
*2 ounces pasta in small shapes
  (little shells or little stars)*
salt
freshly ground black pepper
*1 cup freshly grated parmesan
  cheese*

4. Add carrots to the pot and, 15 minutes later, add the turnips. Five minutes before serving, add the celery, cabbage, and pasta. Add salt and pepper and stir in 2 tablespoons of parmesan cheese. Serve soup with remaining cheese on the side.

NOTE
According to the season, almost any vegetable can be added to a minestrone—peas, green beans, spinach, leeks, zucchini, and so on.

WINE
A valpolicella or other dry, medium-bodied red wine

Bean and Pasta Soup, Roman Style

A variation on the basic minestrone, simple and just as tasty.

1. In a large saucepan, melt the lard and add the salt pork, onion, garlic, and celery; brown well. Add the tomatoes, salt, pepper, warm water, and beans. Cook 5 minutes.

2. Add the elbow macaroni and cook 8 minutes longer. Serve soup in 1 large bowl or individual dishes. Sprinkle some romano cheese overall and pass additional grated cheese.

SERVES 4 TO 6

INGREDIENTS

1 tablespoon leaf lard
⅛ pound salt pork, chopped fine
1 medium onion, chopped fine
1 clove garlic, chopped fine
1 stalk celery, chopped fine
2 fresh tomatoes, peeled, seeded and chopped
1 teaspoon salt
freshly ground black pepper
6 cups warm water
2 cups cooked white beans
1 cup elbow macaroni
freshly grated romano cheese

WINE

A cori rosso (a blend of 2 local Roman grapes with montepulciano) or a chianti classico

Beans and Pasta, Venetian Style

Similar to minestrone, this version emphasizes ham and pork with red beans.

1. Choose a soup pot with a tight cover. Heat the oil in the pot and sauté the pork rind and salt pork until they just begin to turn color and have rendered some fat.

2. Add the beans, onion, cinnamon, ham bone or prosciutto piece, pepper, and water. Bring mixture to a boil, lower heat, and simmer for 2½ hours or until the beans are tender.

SERVES 4 TO 6

INGREDIENTS

2 tablespoons olive oil
½ pound fresh pork rind, cut into ¼-inch cubes
⅛ pound salt pork, cut into ¼-inch cubes
1 cup dried red kidney beans
1 large onion, chopped
⅛ teaspoon cinnamon
1 ham bone, or a strip of prosciutto, ¼-inch thick and 2 by 2-inches wide
freshly ground black pepper
6 cups water
1½ cups small pasta, or string pasta, cut into 1- to 2-inch pieces
salt
freshly grated parmesan cheese

3. Add the pasta pieces and cook for 5 to 10 minutes until the pasta is *al dente*. The cooking time will depend on size and thickness of the pasta. Adjust seasoning by adding some salt if necessary. Remove ham bone or prosciutto and serve soup in a large bowl or in individual bowls. Pass the parmesan cheese to sprinkle on top.

WINE

A pinot grigio or other light-bodied white wine

Bean and Pasta Soup

This is the classic Pasta e Fagioli.

1. In a large saucepan or stock-pot, heat the oil over medium heat and sauté the onion until it begins to turn color. Add the carrot, celery, and pork ribs and sauté for 10 minutes, turning the vegetables and meat every few minutes. Add tomatoes. Lower heat and cook for 10 minutes.

2. Shell the beans, if you are using fresh ones, and rinse them in cold water. Add to the soup pot and stir several times. Then add the stock, cover the pot, and adjust the heat so the liquid is bubbling at a simmer. Simmer for about 50 minutes to 1 hour or until the beans are tender. If you are using precooked beans, cook the tomatoes for 20 minutes instead of 10, as indicated in step 1, and then add the drained beans. Allow the beans to cook in the tomatoes for 5 minutes, always

SERVES 6

INGREDIENTS

¼ cup olive oil
½ onion, chopped (about 2 tablespoons)
1 medium carrot, scraped and chopped fine
1 stalk celery including leaves, strings removed, and chopped fine
4 pork ribs, or 2 pork chops or a ham bone
¾ cup chopped canned Italian plum tomatoes, with their juice
2 pounds fresh cranberry beans (unshelled weight)
3 cups beef stock, fresh or canned
salt
freshly ground black pepper
½ pound egg pasta (page 9) cut into maltagliati shapes, or 6 ounces dried tubular pasta such as elbows
½ cup freshly grated parmesan cheese

stirring, and then add the stock and bring to a simmer.

3. Transfer ½ cup of the beans from the soup pot to a food mill or blender and purée. Return the purée to the soup pot. Add salt and pepper to taste. Add more stock if the soup is too thick. Then add the pasta and, if you are using fresh egg pasta, do not cook longer than 1 minute. If you are using dried pasta, cook until *al dente*. Allow the soup to rest for 10 minutes before serving. Serve grated cheese alongside.

NOTE
If fresh beans are not available, use 1 cup dried great northern beans and cook as directed on the package, or add a drained 20-ounce can of white kidney beans.

WINE
A young chianti or other red wine

Lentil and Pasta Soup

1. Check the dried lentils carefully to remove any foreign matter such as tiny stones or pebbles. To do this, put the lentils in a colander (the flat type is preferable for this), and swirl the lentils around by hand. Then wash them several times by holding the colander under running water.

2. In a large saucepan, heat the butter and oil and sauté the onion until it turns to a light golden color. Add the carrot and the celery and sauté for 3 minutes more, stirring from time to time. Add the pancetta pieces and sauté for 1 minute more. Then add the tomatoes and lower the heat so they cook at a gentle simmer for 25 minutes uncovered. From time to time stir with a wooden fork or spoon.

SERVES 6

INGREDIENTS

*½ pound dried lentils,
 washed and drained*
3 tablespoons butter
3 tablespoons olive oil
1 small onion, chopped fine
1 small carrot, chopped fine
*1 small stalk celery, chopped
 fine*
*1 slice pancetta, cut into
 ¼-inch dice (to make
 about ⅓ cup), or
 prosciutto or unsmoked
 ham*
*1 cup finely chopped canned
 Italian plum tomatoes*
6 cups beef stock
salt
freshly ground black pepper
1 cup small pasta
*1 cup freshly grated parmesan
 cheese*

3. Add the lentils and mix with the other ingredients in the pan. Add the stock and adjust the salt seasoning and add the pepper. Cover and simmer until the lentils are tender; this will take about 45 minutes, but you should taste along the way to avoid overcooking them. Some lentils will absorb a large amount of liquid and this may startle you when you look into the pan. If this happens, just add more stock or broth (even water) to the soup, as you don't want it too thick.

4. Cook the pasta until *al dente,* drain, and add it to the lentil soup. Serve the soup hot in a large bowl or in individual soup bowls, and serve the parmesan cheese separately.

WINE
A buttafuoco or another medium-bodied red wine

Escarole and Pasta Soup

Scarola is a member of the chicory family. There are as many ways to cook it as there are leaves in a head of escarole, and our parents and grand-parents proved this to us over and over. If cooked too plainly it will have little or no taste, but we have had it as a vegetable preparation aggressively flavored with garlic. In this soup the escarole combines with pasta—a happy, mellow-tasting soup to please all members of any family.

1. Separate the escarole leaves from the head and discard any which are inferior. Put the rest in a large saucepan filled with cold water and 1 tablespoon of salt. Leave them this way for 15 or 20 minutes. Remove the leaves and set aside in a colander. Discard water and repeat the process until the leaves are thoroughly clean. Drain and cut the leaves into ½-inch-wide strands and set aside.

2. In a large saucepan or stock-pot, heat the butter and sauté the

SERVES 6

INGREDIENTS

1 pound fresh escarole
salt
¼ cup butter
¼ cup finely chopped onions
4 cups rich chicken stock
1 cup uncooked little star
pasta (stellini) or other
small pasta such as
bowties
freshly grated parmesan
cheese

WINE

A soave or other medium-bodied white wine

onion until nicely browned. Add the escarole strips and a dash of salt. Sauté the escarole for 2 or 3 minutes, stirring it 2 or 3 times. Then add 1 cup of the stock or broth, cover the pot, and cook over very low heat until the esca-role is tender. Depending on the freshness of the escarole, this may take only 20 minutes, but it could take as long as 40 minutes.

3. When the escarole is cooked, add the remaining stock or broth, increase the heat a little and put the cover back on. Bring soup to a boil, add the pasta and cover again. Cook a few minutes, stirring from time to time, until the pasta is *al dente*.

4. Remove soup from the heat, adjust seasoning, and serve in 1 large bowl or in individual bowls, accompanied with freshly grated parmesan cheese.

Chicken Soup with Tagliolini

One of the best ways to use homemade pasta.

1. Put the chicken, veal bones, and giblets (use liver for another purpose) in a large pot with 3 quarts of water. Turn the heat on high, and let the chicken and veal come to a fast boil. Skim the froth that rises to the top. Lower the heat, and add the onion, carrots, celery with leaves, parsley, leek, and tomato. Simmer for about 2 hours.

2. Remove cooked chicken with veal bones and giblets to a large bowl. Set aside and allow to cool. Remove all vegetables from souppot; put through a food mill and purée. Transfer the purée to the chicken stock. Let the soup cool completely. (Put the soup in

On the preceding pages: Pasta Primavera (recipe on page 100); Penne Wrapped in Phyllo (recipe on page 163).

SERVES 6

INGREDIENTS

3½- to 4-pound chicken
1 pound small veal bones
1 large onion
2 carrots, cleaned and left whole
2 stalks celery, cleaned and left whole and including some leaves
6 sprigs fresh parsley, or 1 tablespoon frozen, or 1 teaspoon dried
1 large leek, washed and cut in ½-inch pieces
1 large fresh tomato, peeled, seeded, and chopped into 1-inch pieces; or 1 cup Italian plum tomatoes, seeded and chopped
¼ pound tagliolini
salt
freshly ground black pepper
1 cup freshly grated parmesan cheese

the refrigerator for a few hours but overnight is better.) When the fat has solidified, remove it from the top.

3. Skin and bone the chicken. Remove the breast, cut into large pieces, and set aside. Discard the veal bones. Discard the chicken neck and chop the remaining giblets and add to the breast pieces. (Save the rest of the chicken for another use.) To serve, heat the chicken stock to the boiling point, add the tagliolini and cook until *al dente* (about 5 minutes). Add the chicken and giblet pieces, salt, and freshly ground pepper. Pass the parmesan cheese.

WINE
A trebbiano di romagna or other dry, medium-bodied white wine

Chicken Broth with Capelvenere

The thinnest of pastas makes this soup extra-special. An easy, elegant, lovely soup.

1. In a large saucepan, bring the chicken stock to the boiling point. Add the carrot, celery, and onion and simmer for 8 minutes.

2. Add the pasta all at once and stir immediately into the broth so all strands are separated. Cook for about 6 to 8 minutes. These noodles cook quickly, so check

SERVES 6 TO 8

INGREDIENTS
3 quarts chicken stock or broth
1/2 cup finely cubed carrot, about 1/4-inch
1/2 cup finely cubed celery pieces, about 1/4-inch
1/2 cup finely cubed onion, about 1/4-inch
1/3 pound capelvenere (maidenhair pasta)
salt
freshly ground black pepper
1 cup freshly grated parmesan cheese

even before 6 minutes to be sure they are *al dente*. The vegetables should be *al dente* also. Adjust for seasoning and serve in individual bowls or a large soup bowl. Parmesan cheese should be passed in a separate bowl.

WINE
A riesling from Friuli or another medium-bodied white wine

Chicken Broth with Grated Pasta Mushrooms and Sliced

SERVES 6 TO 8

INGREDIENTS
*¾ pound fresh pasta dough
  (page 9)*
½ pound fresh mushrooms
3 quarts chicken broth
*¼ cup finely chopped Italian
  parsley*
*¼ cup freshly grated
  parmesan cheese*

1. Make the pasta dough and keep it in the ball form. Cover it and let it rest for 15 minutes. Using the back of a cheese grater, grate the pasta ball, add a little flour to keep the grated pasta dry. When all the pasta is grated, combine again with the flour and leave on a plate or flat work surface for approximately 45 minutes.

2. Wipe the mushroom caps with a damp cloth and trim the stem ends. Slice thinly and set aside.

3. In a large saucepan, bring the chicken broth to a boil. Lower the heat and add the grated pasta. Cook for about 8 minutes.

4. Add the mushroom slices and parsley and simmer over low heat for 4 minutes. Serve in 1 large soup bowl or individual soup bowls and sprinkle with freshly grated parmesan cheese.

WINE
A trebbiano d'Arbruzzo or other dry white wine

Small Shells, Chick Peas and Rosemary Soup

Some things are meant to be together; these ingredients prove it.

1. Soak the chick peas in water for several hours or overnight. Rinse and put in a large saucepan, cover with fresh water, add the salt and the rosemary, and cook covered for almost 1 hour or until tender.

2. Drain the chick peas, discard the rosemary, and put the chick peas and liquid through a food mill or process in a food processor in batches. When puréed, set aside.

3. In a large saucepan, heat the oil in a skillet and sauté the garlic and anchovies until they are well blended. Add the tomatoes and chicken broth and bring to the boil. Lower the heat, then simmer for 30 minutes.

SERVES 6

INGREDIENTS

1 pound dried chick peas
1 teaspoon salt
3 sprigs fresh rosemary, tied in a cheesecloth bag
3 tablespoons olive oil
2 cloves garlic, peeled and chopped fine
4 anchovy filets, drained and chopped coarsely
2 medium tomatoes, peeled, seeded, and cubed
2 quarts chicken broth
½ cup small pasta shells

4. In another saucepan, cook the small shells until *al dente*. Drain well and add them to the soup along with the chick peas. Simmer for just 2 minutes and serve in individual bowls or 1 large soup tureen.

WINE
A sauvignon from Friuli or another dry white wine

Green Pea Soup with Pastina

A thick, creamy soup full of wonderful tastes.

1. In a saucepan, add the onion, carrot, celery, and 2 tablespoons of butter. Cover loosely with a piece of wax paper and cook gently until vegetables are limp, about 3 minutes. Stir a few times, and make sure the vegetables do not brown.

2. Transfer the vegetables to a large pan or a casserole with a lid. Add the ham, chicken stock, peas, and thyme and let the soup come to a fast boil. Lower the heat, cover loosely, and simmer for 30 minutes or until the vegetables are tender.

3. Let the soup cool just enough to handle. Remove the ham and put the pea soup through a food mill. Turn, turn, turn, turn, until only the skins of the peas are left in the food mill.

SERVES 4 TO 5

INGREDIENTS

1 large onion, chopped fine
1 large carrot, chopped fine
1 stalk celery with leaves,
*   chopped fine*
4 tablespoons butter
¼ cup finely diced ham
3 cups chicken stock
3 cups fresh or frozen peas
*   (not canned)*
1 teaspoon finely chopped
*   fresh thyme or ½ teaspoon*
*   dried*
½ cup heavy cream
salt to taste
½ cup pastina pasta
freshly ground black pepper

Return the soup to the pot in which it cooked. Slowly add the cream and heat just to the boiling point. Keep hot.

4. Bring 8 cups of water to a rolling boil. Add salt and pasta and cook for 10 or 12 minutes (or follow instructions on package) until the pasta is cooked *al dente*. Drain well and return the pasta to the pan in which it cooked. Add the butter and mix well, then add the pasta to the soup. Taste, and adjust the seasoning.

NOTE
Before putting the peas through the food mill, you might wish to reserve about ¼ cup and add to the soup at the end to give it a slight texture.

WINE
A sauvignon from Venice or any other dry white wine

Pasta in Consommé with Pesto

Clear broth gets a wallup by adding some pesto. A sophisticated soup that always brings praise.

1. In a large saucepan, heat the stock and bring it to a boil. Add the pasta and cook it until *al dente*.

SERVES 4 TO 6

INGREDIENTS
8 cups chicken or beef stock
1 cup small pasta
2 tablespoons Pesto Sauce
*   (page 44)*
1 cup freshly grated parmesan
*   cheese*

2. Remove the soup from the heat and stir in the pesto. Serve soup in a large or individual soup bowls and pass the freshly grated parmesan cheese.

WINE
A Tyrolian riesling or other medium-bodied white wine

Bavette Soup

In Genoa, bavette *are thin and fine noodles, so light and delicious to eat. You won't find these in every pasta shop, but if you do, buy them and make this easy, tasty soup.*

1. In a large saucepan over high heat bring the beef stock to the boil. Add the marjoram, lower the heat, and let it simmer for 3 minutes. Add the noodles, and cook until *al dente.*

INGREDIENTS
1 quart beef stock or canned bouillon
3 leaves fresh marjoram, or 1 teaspoon dried
½ pound bavette noodles
1 egg
salt
freshly ground pepper to taste
3 tablespoons freshly grated parmesan cheese

2. While the pasta is cooking, lightly beat the egg in a small bowl. Add 3 or 4 tablespoons of beef broth to the egg, then add the salt, pepper, and parmesan cheese. Add the egg mixture to the soup and cook for 2 minutes. Serve hot in 4 individual bowls.

WINE
A chianti classico or other medium-bodied red wine

Crespelle with Chives in Broth

The combination of textures here is fascinating.

1. Heat the stock in a large pan or casserole and let it come to a slow boil.

2. Put in the center of each crespelle 1 teaspoon of cheese and a pinch of chives. Roll up crespelle.

SERVES 6

INGREDIENTS
6 cups veal stock
12 Crespelle (page 24)
½ to 1 cup grated asiago cheese
¼ cup chopped fresh chives, or 1½ teaspoons dried freshly grated nutmeg

3. Place crespelle seamside down into an attractive tureen or large bowl. Very carefully ladle the soup onto the rolled crespelle and sprinkle a little nutmeg on top. Serve while still hot.

WINE
A merlot from Venice or another dry, medium-bodied red wine

PASTA MACHINES—
A PRACTICAL COMPARISON

*O*ne of the best pasta machines is the simplest; we have one, and we think it's a helpful tool and so easy to use. Ours is *Rollecta 64,* made in Torino, Italy, but it may be difficult to find. There are other manufacturers of this type pasta machine and they are excellent too, including Atlas. All of them are inexpensive, easy to care for, and last a lifetime. Never wash them; just wipe clean, then flour the rollers. Of all pasta machines, these are the *macchine per fare la pasta* (machines to make pasta).

There are fancier, more expensive pasta makers, but when you get right down to it, the Rollecta 64 and its sister machines are best for us and probably for you, too. These pasta machines are fitted with smooth rollers that will produce several thicknesses of sheet (which is what pasta dough is called when it has been rolled out, whether by hand or by machine). A knob can be turned to widen or narrow the opening between the smooth rollers. (Our machine has 6 settings.) Cutting rollers, which can be attached to the machine, slice the sheet to the noodle width of your desire. Pasta machines are usually fitted with 2-mm and 6-mm cutting rollers. (The 2 cutting rollers are attached to the machine in a single piece.) Additional rollers of 1.5-mm, 4-mm, and 12-mm widths are also available. Only one pasta width may be cut at a time.

Bialetti's has a machine called *La Superautomatica* "Pasta Now." It is an excellent, all-in-one electric pasta machine and is fast and easy to use—also very easy to clean. The ingredients are measured into a piece of equipment called "Pasta Now." It mixes and extrudes the dough in 10 different shapes, depending upon the plate fitted to the nozzle; it will produce classic pasta of various thicknesses and widths, even hollow shapes, such as bucatini and maccheroni. Each part detaches to be easily washed in warm, soapy water. It is very well made and it comes with full instructions and recipes. Its size is approximately 12 by 5½ by 9½ inches.

Pasta Matic is made by Simac. It is a full-cycle machine to make your own pasta at home. One simply puts the properly measured ingredients into the machine and turns it on. And just in a matter of minutes all the ingredients are automatically mixed, kneaded, shaped, and extruded from the machine. The Pasta Matic is easy to use and does not require any special maintenance. A thermal relay will stop the machine after about 25 minutes, which will automatically start up again after 10 minutes. The manufacturer suggests a 30-minute interval between 1 cycle and the next to allow the motor to cool and to allow the extruder to be cleaned. One good thing about this machine is that the pasta mix can be corrected several times and will still make a good pasta. The booklet of directions for this machine is extremely thorough and includes special instructions on how to make potato gnocchi and many other pasta products. There are 15 discs that come with this machine and includes a disc for chitarre (a string pasta that is square, unlike the rounded spaghetti), capellini, bucatino-rigato, bucato, and sfoglia. (Capellini is a very thin spaghetti, bucatino-rigato is a ribbed hollow macaroni, bucato is the same as bucatino-rigato with the ribs, sfoglia are very wide noodles, like lasagne strips.)

Kitchen Aid Food Preparer, one of the best pieces of equipment in any kitchen, has a spaghetti noodle-maker attachment that can make thin and thick spaghetti, flat noodles, macaroni, and lasagne. We have the attachment, and we use it and find it is good. Our only complaint has to do with the seemingly difficult task of cleaning the pasta plates. An instrument akin to a sharp, long needle is provided, but it's not a joy to pierce even spaghetti holes in the plate. Hobart, the manufacturer, however, more than makes up for this by having designed a fine working attachment with a beautiful instructional and recipe booklet—beautiful not in the graphic sense, but in the ease of instructions plus the good menus which will get anyone off to a start in pasta preparation and cooking.

MAIL-ORDER SOURCES FOR PASTA-MAKING EQUIPMENT

MANGANARO'S
488 Ninth Avenue
New York, NY 10036
212-563-5331

BLOOMINGDALE'S
1000 Third Avenue
New York, NY 10022
212-705-2000

SPIEGEL (Catalog order)
1903 W. Pershing Road
Chicago, IL 60609
312-986-1088

MACY'S
Herald Square
New York, NY 10001
212-736-5151

BRIDGE KITCHENWARE CORP.
214 East 52nd Street
New York, NY 10022
212-688-4220

ZABAR'S
249 West 80th Street
New York, NY 10024
212-787-2000

WILLIAMS SONOMA
(Catalog order)
P.O. Box 7456
San Francisco, CA 94120
415-652-9007

DeFRANCISCI MACHINE CORP.
280 Wallabout Street
Brooklyn, NY 11206
212-963-6000

INDEX